The Ground and Nature of the Right

WOODBRIDGE LECTURES

DELIVERED AT COLUMBIA UNIVERSITY

NUMBER FIVE

The Ground and Nature of the Right

CLARENCE IRVING LEWIS

COLUMBIA UNIVERSITY PRESS · NEW YORK 1955

Preface

EXCEPT FOR a few passages, omitted in the oral presentation, this series of the Woodbridge Lectures is printed as delivered at Columbia University in November, 1954.

Any theory of ethics must largely turn upon its treatment of the two major concepts, the good and the right. Both of these have wider application than is involved in questions of morals, but any study of them in their wider scope is bound to be relevant and may be helpful. For appraisals of the good or valuable, I have essayed such examination in Book III of *An Analysis of Knowledge and Valuation*. A general study of the right and the diverse modes in which right and wrong are judged would represent an incomparably greater undertaking, hardly to be accomplished except by embracing an adequate theory of all the normative disciplines. What is attempted here is a collation of fundamental considerations, particularly such as bear upon ethics, together with suggested conclusions which I think more extended examination would support.

Some points here advanced were first put forward in a paper contributed to the volume *Vision and Action,* presented to Horace M. Kallen on his seventieth birthday. I am indebted to its editor, Professor Sidney Ratner, and to the Rutgers University Press for their inclusion of that paper with the understanding that fuller treatment of its topic, at a later date, was contemplated.

The materials from which the content of these lectures was drawn have profited from the opportunities for study and discussion afforded by my appointment as John Grier Hibben Research Fellow in Philosophy at Princeton University in 1953–54.

My thanks are due to the Department of Philosophy in Columbia University for their many kind offices in connection with the lectures and for their help in bringing the lectures to publication.

C. I. Lewis

Stanford, California
February 8, 1955

Contents

Woodbridge Lectures

AT his death in 1940 Professor Frederick Woodbridge left a bequest to Columbia University for the purpose of bringing distinguished philosophers to the University from time to time and for making their lectures available through publication. Some of Professor Woodbridge's friends made substantial additions to this bequest, and thus made it possible for the late President Butler to establish the Woodbridge Memorial Fund. The Woodbridge Lectures are delivered triennially. All these series have been published in book form by the Columbia University Press.

1. Wilmon H. Sheldon, *Process and Polarity*
2. George Plimpton Adams, *Man and Metaphysics*
3. Sterling Power Lamprecht, *Nature and History*
4. Harry Todd Costello,
    A Philosophy of the Real and the Possible
5. Clarence Irving Lewis, *The Ground and Nature of the Right*

The Ground and Nature of the Right

•

Modes of Right and Wrong

IN ALL the world and in all of life there is nothing more important to determine than what is right. Whatever the matter
which lies before us calling for consideration, whatever the
question asked or the problem to be solved, there is some set-
tlement of it which will meet the situation and is to be sought
as well as various other ways in which it might be fronted
which would fail to satisfy the requirements. Otherwise the
issue would be unreal or else insoluble; either no consideration
would be called for except to clear away our own confusions,
or else no consideration we could give would avail us anything. Wherever there is a decision to be made or any deliberation is in point, there is a right determination of the matter in
hand which is to be found and adhered to, and other possible
commitments which would be wrong and are to be avoided.
To say that a thing is right is simply to characterize it as
representing the desiderated commitment or choice in any

situation calling for deliberate decision. What is right is thus the question of all questions; and the distinction of right and wrong extends to every topic of reflection and to all that human self-determination of act or attitude may affect.⟩

These truths are so simple and so obvious that pronouncement of them comes near to saying nothing. What might be doubtful concerning right and wrong and stand in need of clarification, appears hardly to be touched by such generalities. But whatever these further and real issues, this pervasiveness of our required concern for right and wrong, in some one or another of their senses, and our unavoidable involvement with something which these words connote as often as we think to any conclusion or decide any action, would seem to be sufficient for prima-facie presumption that the distinction itself is real and ultimate and touches something fixed in the nature of things and impossible to repudiate.

⟨We might, then, expect to begin at once with matters which are more specific—of the morally right or of the legally or politically right—making no question of the comprehensive meaning of right and wrong or of the nature and ground of the right at large. We live, however, in an age of skepticism—a period in which our civilization has undergone changes which have been so radical and have occurred within a time historically so short that there is hardly anything which has been left undisturbed and may be regarded as well settled. Men have become doubtful of any bedrock for firm belief, any final ground for unhesitant action, and of any principles not relative to circumstance or colored by personal feeling or affected by persuasions which may be only temporary and local.⟩ And in this period, as in other and like epochs in history, doubts are voiced whether the distinction of right and wrong, in one or another of its modes, is other than subjective or has any fixed and final sense.

Perhaps we should also acknowledge that there is something in this attitude of doubt that stops at nothing, and leaves no root for firm conviction, the significance of which is not confined to periods of ferment and of crisis like the present. In some part this may be a price we pay for progress, for universal education and democracy; an inevitable side-product of our ruling principle that every man must think for himself, and that there is no dictum nor any accepted shibboleth which he may not challenge. If we are to cherish and further realize these ideals which are basic for our Western mores then we must, perhaps, learn to live with such recurrent skepticism and with the fact that nothing is ever so well settled that question of it will not be raised again.

If that be the case, however, and if we are to continue in the direction in which European and American thought has moved since the Age of Enlightenment, or even since the time of Socrates, and if we are not to lapse into some authoritarianism and a submergence of the individual in a mass-mind, then it seems clear that there are two further lessons which we must take to heart and grasp more firmly. We must learn that, both in our individual thinking and in our corporate decisions, perennial reconsideration and reappraisal must not run to the length of intellectual self-frustration and practical abulia. They must not render us incapable of firm commitment in exigent circumstances. Questions are pointless if decision is impossible. And when the question is one of action, some resolution of it is unavoidable. The occasion for action arises, and will pass; and failure of decision is itself a manner of deciding since it resigns that opportunity to affect the issue which lay open to us.

Second, we must recognize that the questioning attitude itself has its own presumptions; and these are such as to make the validity of our general sense of right and wrong the last thing that could be doubted. Concerning almost anything else, finality of conviction, beyond any need to reconsider, might reasonably be challenged. But if there be no right and wrong, then doubt itself as well as any resolution of it becomes meaningless.

To have a question or a problem presumes that there is an answer or solution; otherwise, as we have noted, the issue becomes less than genuine. But this is not to presume that the solution of every inquiry will be readily open to us or that in usual circumstances the best solution we can reach will be one which never after need be reconsidered. We are familiar with the perennial fact of our ignorance, by reason of which we often must decide according to the weight of the evidence which is open to us, though it is insufficient for finality. Doubt, in such cases, performs its vital function by reminding us that our ignorance may be curable or that second thought may find more which is at hand and pertinent than we have noted. Doubt also warns us to proceed warily, holding ourselves open to revision of belief or attitude and to any correction of our decision which might not come too late. These are matters we must look further into at a later point. They mark a distinction between what is justified as the best decision we can take and that ideal which never-ending inquiry takes as its permanent goal. The reasonably credible and the absolute truth are two different things, and justified decisions, like probabilities, are relative to our ignorance. If the skeptic were to remind us merely that the absolute truth is not vouchsafed to us, we might think he takes in too much territory but still admit that he performs a useful office. But that would not be skepticism. What the skeptic tells us is that our ignorance is incurable, or that our inquiry itself is unmeaning. In that case, doubt exercises no useful function; one proposed solution is as good, or as bad, as another, and to doubt is as pointless as to inquire. We might best forget the whole matter—if that be possible.

There are some matters upon which men have spent time which might, indeed, as well or better be forgotten. But the distinction of right and wrong could not possibly be amongst them. Any chronic disbeliever who chooses the common conviction on that point as his target could not have made a poorer choice. For skepticism does not solve the problem addressed but abolishes it, leaving nothing to be done about it and every decision of it pointless. And here the skeptic is hoist by his own petard. Skepticism is itself one possible conviction, one attitude, one alternative of response to whatever general issue is in question. And the skeptic either maintains that his attitude is the right one or he asserts nothing. Without a right to be sought and adhered to and a wrong to be avoided, the skeptic could not be right and those who disagree with him could not be wrong; and if in fact he should be right then nobody could be right and nobody could be wrong, and there would be no issue.

It will be objected to this, I am sure, that there is indeed no issue of the sort here put because the skeptic so far spoken of is a man of straw, and none has ever challenged the distinction of right and wrong in every sense of these words. Perhaps it will also be said that the above is merely confusing by reason of using the words "right" and "wrong" in an indefensibly ambiguous manner—to cover rightness and wrongness in the determination of belief, which ought to be discussed in other terms such as "truth" and "falsity"; and to cover also all manner of right and wrong doing, which should be subject to distinctions.

The first of these objections comes near to being true: one must go back to Protagoras and the ancient Cynics to find a clear case of skepticism extending to all problems and all departments of investigation. Hume, who was skeptical of empirical knowledge, did not challenge the distinction between morally right and morally wrong; and those who have been skeptical of the moral distinctions have commonly raised no question of the validity of science and knowledge in general.

It may be important nevertheless to point out this predicament into which any who would challenge the distinction of right and wrong in general must fall. A minor reason is that those who are skeptical of the moral distinction or of any objective rightness or wrongness of value assessments, or of both of these, have sometimes so written as to allow an unwary reader to suppose that every veridical sense of these terms, and integrity in general, are at stake in their discussions; and have failed to delimit, with sufficient care, the field to which their skeptical doubt is meant to be confined. A more important reason—and one which is pertinent to the second objection also —is that it can be doubted whether this skepticism of the moral, or moral and valuational, *can* be successfully delimited so as to avoid implication of a skepticism which is more general, and in consequence self-defeating. We must raise the question at least whether there could be rightness in believing and affirming but no implication contained in that of objective rightness in decision of what we do; or whether there could be objective rightness in our drawing of conclusions but none in valuations made; or whether acts could be rightly or wrongly directed to self-interested ends with no implication in that of a required respect for the ends of others.

It would be a little incredible—would it not—that the various ways in which men have applied these same terms, "right" and "wrong," should have no part of their significance which is common, and that there are no mutual implications between right believing and concluding, right valuing, and right doing; or between right pursuit of personal ends and right conduct toward our fellows. Already, we have suggested such a common connotation included in the various more specific senses of "right" and "wrong"; the significance of a desiderated commitment in any matter to be decided. The field of judgment of right and wrong extends to whatever is subject to human deliberation or calls for decision. And a meaning which is thus general is not thereby ambiguous, even when it is inexplicit or stands in need of elucidation. We can hope for any needed clarification, and anticipate that if it be achieved, something of import for more specific senses, and any relations which these have to one another, may be contained in that. It is in such hope that our further study here is undertaken.

Most frequently it is the moral signification of "right" as opposed to "wrong" which comes first to mind. It is the moral problems which are most commonly and most seriously pursued under that title; and one who announces "the right" as his topic is expected to speak of our conduct toward one another and of justice. We seem sometimes to forget that there is right and wrong not only about paying debts and keeping promises, but about adding a column of figures, or building a wall, or drawing a conclusion; about making an investment, playing a game, choosing one's vocation, filling out a tax-return, regulating our diet. And if it is true that any of these activities might be, under some circumstances or in some aspect of it, invested with a moral significance, it is still doubtful that the rightness or wrongness so attributed is one which answers to moral principles rather than to rules or interests of some other kind. We do indeed vaguely discern a very wide sense of "moral" in which it extends to every mode of our self-government and may significantly apply to anything we do and all we may affect; to everything concerning which there is any sense of ought or ought-not. Still that is not the usual significance of "moral"; the morally right is one species of right and cannot forthwith be identified with right in general.

It is indeed what pertains to morals and to ethics which is our main interest here. And it is also the distinction of moral right from moral wrong which takes the brunt of that skepticism which has been mentioned, and is charged with being subjective or emotive only, or merely relative to the cultural context, or a bourgeois superstition. But if it is the morally right whose nature and validity are most important and have received most attention, still it would be an oversight to proceed as if the qualification "moral" were simply pleonasm and moral distinctions cover the whole range of right and wrong.

It is, moreover, less clear than one might suppose just what area it is within which moral distinctions apply. One might expect that students of ethics would at least agree as to their topic; otherwise, how can they disagree? But examination of historic ethical theories reveals no such unanimity. It does, to be sure, come near to being generally agreed that rightness or wrongness of overt and deliberate acts, assessed by reference to their actual or expected effects of good or ill to persons other than the doer, is the major point of ethical investigation— though historic theories and authors could be cited to put even that in doubt. But if we ask what else, if anything, is essentially included in the scope of ethical inquiry, then diversity rather than unanimity shows itself to be the rule. We may—even must —for example, ask whether prudential action and decision of it, where any effect upon others is at a minimum, is to be included amongst the topics of ethics, and whether what is justified as adjudged on the basis of self-interest is to be taken as a kind of moral rightness, and questions of prudence as representing one type of moral problem. If we say "Yes," we are confronted with Kant who denies all moral worth to prudentially motivated action.* And if we say "No," we do violence to Bentham, who finds no motive save the prudential to which humans are capable of responding, and hence no content for moral assessment by any other standard than eventual self-interest.

That the prudential mode of judging acts is different from their assessment as just to others, must be granted if we admit that prudent acts may sometimes be unjust, or that some which are just contravene the dictate of self-interest. And if it be not granted without argument that the prudential assessment is a required mode of judgment, then it should be sufficient to point

---

*Except in the rather far-fetched sense that temptation to do ill to others may be aggravated by finding ourselves in an evil case, and it is a duty to avoid such temptation so far as may be.

out that none of us could well determine what justice dictates unless we be able to weigh the interests of others—their self-interest. Conversely, if the doer's own interest be not already included in what just action must depend upon, the just man could hardly have any ground for judging the interests of others if he lacked the capacity to judge his own. If it does not go without saying that one ought to be prudent—as prudent, let us say, as justice to others will allow—then it should require no more than the question why we are so concerned to inculcate prudence as well as justice in our children, to assure the point that prudence is some kind of dictate, sanctioning some acts and prohibiting others, and that the distinction of the prudentially right and wrong is autonomous and distinct from that of justice and has some manner of its own validity.

The question of the relation between prudence and justice is an inevitable topic of ethics; and the questions of prudent behavior, apart from or beyond the questions of justice, constitute an inevitable problem of human life. Whether questions of the prudentially sanctioned as such are moral issues, would seem to depend mainly upon how one chooses to delimit application of the term "moral." To exclude them from ethics is possibly justified in the interest of the separation of problems. That, however, seems dubious: one could also think that such exclusion masks a derogation of the actual importance of prudential behavior or betokens an overweening inclination to the edifying. In any case, the prudential questions are problems of right conduct and, if excluded from ethics, must find their place in the larger topic of practical philosophy (or philosophy of practice), concerned with principles of our rational self-government of action.

Questions of the technically right—how to do so and so or how to achieve some particular species of common purposes—may also call for separate consideration. Such questions constitute a part of the theory of any art or the critique of any professional practice. These are of a mixed sort and are normative only in a sense which is peculiar to this mode of the right and wrong. There may or may not be a question of right doing in the undertaking of a given technical or professional task; but having undertaken it, one finds it imperative to carry it through in ways which are technically correct or professionally justified. Somewhat similarly, there may or may not be some rightness or wrongness in the individual's commitment to a vocation in question, or in the practice of it by those who lack the technical or professional training and competence. But in any case those who commit themselves to this vocation—and perhaps those who practice it without assured skill—fall under certain obligations to others, some of which may be peculiar to exercise of the particular social function served by the art or profession in question. In other words, the technical or professional purpose, or the particular vocational project, may or may not be imperative for the individual to choose, and may or may not be imperative for him to avoid; but in any case the manner in which it is pursued or carried out is subject to criticism as technically right and justified or technically wrong and contravening the dictates of such practice.

We should also observe that major questions of right and wrong are not exhausted by those concerned with right doing, in the ordinary sense. Thinking, believing, inferring and concluding, and even imagining, so far as imagination is directed to the interests of some creative purpose, are likewise criticizable as right or wrong. It is also of first importance to remark that the rightness of our doing is essentially connected with rightness in that thinking which constitutes the deliberation of it and controls the decision of action taken. Such thinking is subject to our self-government and represents a kind of activity. There are *ways* of thinking; and it is specific modes of such mental activity, and the acceptance or rejection of that in which it terminates, which are denominated right or wrong. There is logical rightness of conclusions validly related to their premises, and logical wrongness of fallacious inference. There is rightness or wrongness of belief by reference to evidence given or available. There is correctness or incorrectness in any attempt to represent what is absent or undisclosed. And there is justification or the lack of it in any prediction to which we commit ourselves. All these are to be observed in addition to the fact already noted that any deliberate doing represents a decision the determination of which is by some mental process; and the doing itself is right or wrong according as the decision of it is right or wrong.

These are complex matters; and one difficulty of discussing them concerns vocabulary. Such words as "doing," "act," and "activity" are, in common usage, ambiguous, and in order to observe correctly the relation between what they designate and what is subject to the distinction of right and wrong, it will be necessary to restrict ourselves to usages of these terms which are narrower than those which common idiom allows.

First, let us say that any process of consciousness which we are incapable of altering or directing, if it is to be called thinking at all, at least should not be called active thinking; it is, rather, a mode in which we are affected—a "passion" in the orig-

inal sense of that word. Second, though we shall include under
activities all those processes of consciousness which we initiate
or control, let us reserve the word "act" for cases in which
some physical doing is involved. That is, let us use "activity"
as the wider term applicable to any self-governed process,
whether mental or physical or both, but reserve "act" as a narrower designation inapplicable unless something physical is
brought about. We should not overlook the fact, however, that
the results of physical doing are not confined to consequences
which are physical. Unless the parapsychological is to be admitted, we can affect no other consciousness than our own except by overt behavior, if it be only by speech or gesture. But
what we can so bring about includes effects upon the *experience* of others, and such effects upon the lives of other persons
are a most important kind of consequences of action from the
moral point of view.

Third, let us avoid that wide sense of the word "act" in which
it may be applied to any bodily behavior, whether or not it is
subject to our decision and control. Among what are sometimes called acts or activities, in this wide sense of behavior, we
are interested only in those which are right or wrong because
they reflect our initiative and self-direction; and we may restrict our terms here to accord with that interest.

However—and this is a fourth point to be observed—acts and
activities in this restricted sense are not altogether confined to
those which are deliberate in the sense of being deliberated.
Much of what we purposefully do is habitual or semiauto-
matic, and largely "does itself." Our attribution of it to our
own agency turns upon the fact that it is corrigible. Behavior
which consciously comes about with a sense of our assent and

would not have occurred unless we allowed it, is included in that for which we normally accept responsibility. And certainly this is a correct sense of that which we attribute to ourselves. If not deliberated and decided on this occasion, it still represents a way of acting which reflects past deliberations and decisions and has become what we may call an active attitude of ours, which persists because it has at least our acquiescence. This habit or attitude is itself something for which we are responsible. It is not incorrigible but prevails with us because we allow it; because somewhere along the path of its development, and presumably on more than one occasion, this manner of activity has drawn our critical attention and been deliberated and approved. More often than not, any doing which answers to such a continuing active attitude will be called a deliberate act; and it would be inappropriate and impractical to impute responsibility in any narrower way. But the point to observe is that the connection with deliberation and decision, either past or present, is still of the essence of any activity regarded as self-governed.

In this same connection, it may be well to observe in passing that there are other modes of response which also are sometimes spoken of as attitudes. There are, for example, ways of fronting situations which are dominated by uncontrolled impulse or emotion. But these are passions rather than actions. If they are to be called attitudes at all, at least they should not be spoken of as "active" attitudes; "behavioral attitudes" would be a more appropriate term.

It is activities determined directly or indirectly by deliberation and decision, together with what flows from them, for which we are properly accountable and to which criticism is properly addressed. And each and every such piece of our conduct, mental or physical, is either right or wrong. One and all, they are justified or unjustified, commitments validly or invalidly made, correct or incorrect in some sense of these words, or in more than one.

It is such justification of commitments or the lack of it which is the question lying over and above any causal explanation of them as occurrent phenomena or any subsumption of them under the descriptive generalizations of natural law, and which marks them as subject to that kind of investigation and that manner of assessment which is called normative. Such activities constitute the subject matter of those disciplines which, in the history of thought, have tended to remain as departments of philosophical inquiry instead of separating off from philosophy and coming to be regarded as distinct. In the present state of opinion, such normative studies are often denied the status of science altogether, even when the legitimacy of them is not challenged. But whether they be scientific or not, no normal human adult could live five minutes without making such normative assessments; and if he could, his activities would lack any reasonable direction of them and threaten to be pointless. Science itself must presume them, even if it refuses to discuss them. In science as elsewhere, what has not been subjected to critical appraisal and found correct, is unreliable and presumably unimportant.

The modes of such normative critique are obviously various; and until they are distinguished and the specifically different criteria to which they answer have been determined, both what they have in common and what essential relations they may have to one another must likewise remain obscure. So far, we observe only the presumption that whatever is in any sense right or wrong is so regarded by reason of its involvement in our self-directed activities, and as representing some manner of them to be adhered to as justified or warranted or one to be avoided as unjustifiable and contravening that to which we should conform.

Already a major division within the normative in general suggests itself: that between activities which are exclusively mental, such as believing and inferring, and those which involve some physical bringing about—effects we may produce in the ongoing process of the world about us, and particularly effects which have importance either for ourselves or for others. It further suggests itself that this manner of division is coordinate with the two major types of decision which men are called upon to make; determinations as to fact, in our concluding and commitments of belief, and determinations to do, in any attempt we may make to modify what might otherwise take place. It will likewise occur to us that this major division of our activities is pertinent to the two mainly recognized and distinguished branches of normative critique, logic and ethics.

We have already observed, however, that ethics, as usually pursued, does not include the whole topic of our self-governed doing. And we shall similarly find that logic, as usually considered, fails to cover the whole ground of required critical assessment of our mental activities, or even those of thinking and believing. The reasons for this, in both cases, as well as the question whether what ethics and logic so omit is included in some other normative discipline, will be a further matter of interest.

As between these two major divisions of normative assessment, what relates to determinations of fact, to concluding and believing, is naturally prior. There is no decision of action which could reasonably be taken without reference to the external circumstances of it or without foresight of consequences to be expected from adoption of it. Nor could any decision to do be assessed as right or wrong without reference to the doer's beliefs and what is evidenced to him as fact. For that reason, if for no other, any rightness or wrongness of doing is a more complex problem than rightness or wrongness in our mental activities. Though our main interest here will be in what is pertinent to ethics, this complexity of its problems, as well as the natural order observed above, dictates that we begin with consideration of right and wrong in concluding and believing, proceeding to what is more specifically relevant to ethics in later chapters.

Right Believing and Concluding

WHATEVER is decidable or can be determined by deliberation is right or wrong. This distinction extends to all that reflects the possible self-government of agents like ourselves, but does not extend to what lies beyond our control. The significant words here are "responsible," "justified" or "unjustified," "correct" or "incorrect." This represents the strict sense of "right" and "wrong"; and we have so far said little or nothing of any other meaning of these terms. There are, however, various derivative senses also and, although these are matters more appropriate to what comes later, we must take brief notice of some of them now.

As we have seen, deliberation and criticism are broadly correlative terms. When we criticize (critically assess) what we may or might do before deciding between alternatives of action, we call it deliberation; and when we deliberate upon the rightness or wrongness of doing ex post facto, we call it criticism. But if we did not critically assess our possible actions before deciding, the doing would not be deliberate and taken by decision. It is, then, not only the actually done but anything which may be done to which the distinction of right and wrong applies. Similarly, it would be pointless to assess what is already committed as right or wrong if it were not that there will be later and similar occasions when action is to be decided, and our ex post facto critical attitude may be of effect in such future decisions. By the same token, it is well so to criticize not only what was done deliberately but anything which, even if done thoughtlessly or without responsibility on a particular past occasion, may later be a matter for deliberate doing.

Though less important for us here, it may also have explanatory value if we note that though any criticism in the strictest sense is of an agent for his activity, the criticism extends to that for which he is so responsible. It is indeed difficult to speak of acts and activities except by reference to what is so brought about. In consequence, we criticize any result of action as a right or wrong thing to bring about or aim at. And even that which happens in a particular instance without the responsibility of any agent, may be criticized when we think of it as a possible result which might be brought about or purposed by some agent on some hypothetical occasion. If anyone *were* to bring this about deliberately, it would be a right, or a wrong, thing to do. For all these reasons, it is important to assess critically and determine as right or wrong not only that which our activities do affect but almost anything they may or might affect; and from the point of view of critique, the question of a particular agent's responsibility on a particular occasion is most frequently a less important matter.

Such considerations are especially important when we turn to the topic of mental activities; first, because what we can affect and what is beyond our control are so complexly intermingled in our conscious processes, and second, because oftentimes if we think wrongly we can take a second thought before anything irretrievable happens as result of our thinking. Indeed, if it were not for the fact that much of what passes before (or in) our minds calls for nothing in the nature of commitment, and that when this is called for we can give it or withhold it, it might well be impossible to mark off anything appropriately to be called mental activities from mental phenomena in which there is no sense of agency or significance of self-control.

All of what goes on in mind, and any content of the stream of consciousness, is in some sense a datum of fact, open to our self-conscious notice. But these items are of various kinds, characterized by qualities by virtue of which they function differently and have for us modes of significance which are different. By reference to such qualities, they are classifiable as presentations of sense, as memories, as imaginings, as feelings of pleasure and pain, as emotions, as impulses, as feelings of conation, as desires, wishes, purposes, inclinations to do, and in various other ways. Our classification of them in these different ways may sometimes be in error; for example, we may mistake imagining for memory or even for sense presentation. But at least the clues on the basis of which such classifications are to be made must be native qualities of conscious content, there to be observed. The modes in which such items follow upon one another are also various; there is suggestion, free association, the successiveness characteristic of day-dreaming, as well as that which is dominated by point of view, or by a sense of problem and of purpose. Also there is that manner of irruption characteristic of sense and of passive feeling or shock.

Amongst the characteristics of such items and the modes of their succession, there is the distinction of the initiated and the initiatable from that which is not induced or cannot be induced; of the alterable from the inalterable, in the manner of its arising and its persistence or lapsing; of what comes by wish or will and is governed, directed, controllable, from that which is willy-nilly. Here again, such classification of passages of experience may in a particular instance be subject to error; but the clue to it must be in some found character of the classified which is there and open to our observation. Otherwise we could never become aware of the distinction of activity from the passively experienced and learn to make it, or acquire any sense of self-control and hence of our possible control of other things.

All items of conscious content and all features of the mental procession of consciousness are, of course, attributable to ourselves in the sense of being something which happens in our case. But it is this distinction of active passage from passive enduring and the endurance of effect visited, which lies at the bottom of any sense of self in contrast to the non-ego of the external world. Without this contrast of action and passion, it is to be doubted that any sense of self could arise at all.

This distinction marks off what is attributable to us as our own activity from that which happens in our case by reason of what is alien and other; it sets that which arises and persists or lapses amenably to wish and will in contrast to that whose coming about or persisting or passing is felt as something which happens through an agency exercised upon us and other than our own. Our sense of doing as a physical bringing about, is complex. It requires first that something be recognized as external fact, which is as it is and not otherwise, and then the recognition of our actual or possible modification of it. What we call our thinking is those passages of consciousness which, in the manner of their succession, are free of dominance by any recognized alien reality. But if all passage of experience which is not attributable to external realities and the effects of them upon us is in a broad sense thinking, still it requires a further distinction to mark off thinking which is either right or wrong. That it occurs otherwise than as an effect of recognized external entities upon us does not forthwith mark it as self-directed. It may still be ungoverned and, so to say, "do it-self." And further, if like the day-dream, it be amenable to our wish and will, it still may be idle and nonsignificant, untouched by serious purpose. It may not engage us because no portent attaches to it and our awareness of it arouses no concern.

Any full phenomenological account would be beyond us here and run to impermissable length. What particularly must interest us is those passages of consciousness which not only have the broad character of thinking, and the more specific character of governable thought-process, but which also are purposive and affected with a sense of portent or of problem, because they are taken to be directly or indirectly significant of what will or may affect our further experience. These include the processes called cognitive. They are such as may be assigned the significance of representation and invested with a sense of fact or the query of fact. Examination of such thought-processes would, however, show that, even when purposively directed, they are less than completely amenable to our self-government: for example, if I wish to think of the name of a man now approaching me, it may come or it may not come with the requisite sense of the factual. But regardless of what lies within our command and what beyond it, in the eventuation of such thought-processes, there is one feature with respect to which they are, at one and the same time, correct or incorrect and wholly subject to our determination. We either accept or refuse the eventuation of such thinking. We assign objective reference or withhold it. It is thinking in the sense of imagining with assigned objective reference, or at least the query of it, which is representing. And such representation is the essential feature of cognition. If, when this man approaches, the name "Smith" comes to my mind, I accept this suggestion and act on it, or I decide, in view of the manner of its thought-eventuation, that it is unreliable. And if, without justification, I accept it and this leads to a slightly uncomfortable sequel, my responsibility in the matter will be clear. It is in this sense that any result of thinking most clearly represents an activity we exercise and is subject to decision. What we shall think *of,* is partly within our control and partly not; but what we shall think *of it* is our full responsibility.

Perhaps it will be remarked that the above is not only inadequate but definitely faulty, in its suggestion of the manner in which our cognitive determinations as to fact are right or wrong, since much of cognition is not representational and an eventuation of thinking but dominated by the willy-nilly and presentational element of the sense-given in experience. This possible objection, however, would not, I think, be well taken. Some thinking to which objective reference may attach includes both presentational and representational elements, and some may comprise the representational exclusively, but no thinking can have cognitive significance if the representational element is lacking. An apprehension which should stop short with absorption in the sense-given, adding nothing, might be aesthetic in the literal sense but could not be cognitive. A child's titillation with a cadence of sound, for example, may not be affected with any rightness or wrongness because no cognitive significance is assigned to it; but if he interprets this auditory presentation as "hearing the ice-cream cart coming" then, by virtue of the objective reference so involved, his apprehension is either authentic and justified or unwarranted and mistaken. It is the credit attached, and attaching to what we do not sense but represent which is the point of cognitive apprehension. Any knowing must include belief in something not sense-given but credited as authentic. To say that the cognitive element in cognition is always inferential would hardly be precise; but it will be fully correct to say that cognition is always such that any test of its correctness will involve test of some inference implicit in it. A sense-given item of experience may automatically arouse objective belief; but while the givenness of the presentation is an uncontrollable element in experience, the belief is not. The inferential credit attached, even if attachment of it be by spontaneous association, is subject to review and critical second-thinking. For example, if one see a red after-image projected against a white wall and spontaneously think "spot of red paint," it is the attribution of the permanent paint-spot character which is cognitive—and in our example, invalid and illusory. Perception involves both seeing (or otherwise sensing) *and believing*. It is the believing which is cognitive; and the believing is inferential in significance. By the same token, though the seeing is incorrigible, the believing is corrigible, and this perceptual belief is either right or wrong. Criticism of this experience as cognitive—as a justified belief in objective fact or as a momentary illusion to be rejected—is critical assessment of the inference from "seen redness" to "paint-spot on the wall" as a justified conclusion or as a hasty suggestion of thought and an unwarranted belief.

Let us remark also that, as the example just given may suggest, the criticism appropriate to cognition is often such as may more properly be directed on a belief-*attitude* or belief-*habit* rather than upon our momentary acceptance of belief suggested. Too much of our perceptual believing is too spontaneous to be fully governed and hence criticizable, in the particular instance. But our *ways* of attaching or withholding the cognitive assignment of objective fact are subject to criticism, and our too thoughtless acceptance of such a suggestion, invalid as inference from the evidence of sense, is subject to critical review and to self-discipline if this belief-habit be one frequently leading to avoidable error. When the inferential element is more explicit and is represented by a directed train of thought, the criticism may apply to this activity of thinking directly.

To sum up so far, then: Thinking as distinguishable from overt doing, and considered apart from its connection with decisions to do, is right or wrong and criticizable so far as it has the character of governable activity resulting in the assignment of objective reference to representations; the character of a determination of fact; a belief which explicitly or implicitly has the character of inferred conclusion, and as such is justified, warranted and right or unjustified and wrong.

The main mode of such criticism, applicable to cognition, is that which is familiar to us as logic. But if we are so to think of the matter, there are observations about logic itself of which we may do well to remind ourselves. It is somewhat the fashion currently to think of logic simply as a form of truth and deemphasize its significance as critique. But apart from the normative function it may exercise in criticism of our activities of thinking and inferring, logic would be threatened with the triviality of tautologies in general and probably would never have come to be formulated. It arises as a systematization of one form of our critical self-consciousness, directed to test and amendment of one pervasive mode of our self-governed and self-governable activities. It may also be well to remember what an inference is; namely, the passage of thought to an asserted conclusion. Without the affirmation of a belief, there is no inference: the hypothetical formulation of a logical connection involves no inference—unless indeed this hypothetical statement itself be one believed on the ground of its relation to some other and antecedent belief. An inference is a determination of objective fact, rightly or wrongly. We are also too much prone— not the logicians but the rest of us—to think of logic as if it were critique exclusively of those modes of inference which are called deductive and are characterized by a kind of certainty which is, in fact, seldom justified in our thinking outside of mathematics and logic itself. This is the more in point because, as is now generally admitted, no belief in any matter of empirical fact, whether one of our common-sense knowledge or of natural science, could be fully justified by deductive logic, or even by deduction together with the data which presentational experience affords. All such conclusions have inductive assurance only.

If we are to appreciate the significance of this last point for critical assessment perhaps we should remind ourselves of certain familiar facts which go with the distinction of induction from deduction. Deductive conclusions are always as certain as the premises from which they are drawn. If we are sure that all A is B and that all B is C, we are justified in concluding with equal certainty that all A is C. Speaking more generally and putting the matter precisely: a conclusion drawn from given premises according to the rules of deduction is thereby as well assured as the conjoint statement of the premises. The deductive conclusion *may* be one which is *better* assured than its premises—on other grounds—but it *cannot* be *less* well assured. If the conclusion 'R' is deducible from the premises 'P' and 'Q,' and 'P' is certain and 'Q' is certain, so that the conjoint statement 'P and Q' is certain, the conclusion 'R' is thereby rendered certain.

Now take a case in which the premises are not certain but only probable, but the conclusion follows deductively from the premises. In such a case, the conclusion will not—ordinarily— be certain, but it must be at least as probable as the *conjoint statement* of the premises. If today is Monday and tomorrow is fair, then Tuesday this week will be a fair day. That conclusion follows deductively from the premises. If we are certain that today is Monday and certain that tomorrow will be fair, then certainly Tuesday this week will be a fair day. And if we are less than certain of tomorrow's weather and perhaps not quite sure of the day of the week, still "Tuesday this week will be a fair day" must be at least as probable as the conjoint statement, "Today is Monday and tomorrow will be fair." However, we here encounter the complication that when each of two premises is only probable, the conjoint statement of them can—usually will—be less probable than either premise taken separately. If there are three chances out of four that today is Monday, and two chances out of three that tomorrow will be fair, then the probability of the conjoint statement, "Today is Monday *and* tomorrow will be fair," is only one half ($\frac{3}{4} \times \frac{2}{3} = \frac{1}{2}$), which is less than the probability of either premise alone. To see this more quickly, take a different example: If the first throw of this coin is a head and the second throw is a head, then there will be no tail (non-head) on the first two throws. Here likewise, the conclusion is deductive. And the probability of each premise is one-half. But the probability of the *conjoint statement* of the premises, "The first throw will be a head *and* the second throw will be a head," is only one-quarter. But our point still holds: in either of these cases—and in any other—a deductive conclusion is at least as probable as the conjoint statement of its premises.

With induction the case is different. An inductive conclusion drawn from premises which are certain is assured by them as probable only.* And if the conjoint formulation of the premises be itself only probable—and, as we should commonly suppose, all the premises are requisite for the conclusion, and this conclusion is not also *deductively* derivable from them—then the degree of that probability represents the upper limit of the probability so assured to the conclusion.

These considerations have one consequence which may seem small but is in fact of fundamental importance for the char-

---

* We must, of course, exclude here cases which are sometimes *called* induction—"mathematical induction," for example, and what was traditionally called "perfect induction" in which the premises together exhaust all the cases covered in the conclusion. Both of these are in fact particular modes of deductive inference, as is now commonly understood.

acter of any critique which would be applicable to our empirical knowledge. As we have just observed, if a conclusion 'R' follows deductively from a premise 'P' (whether this premise 'P' be simple or complex) then this conclusion 'R' must be at least as probable as 'P.' If "Today is Monday" deductively assures the conclusion "Tomorrow will be Tuesday," then add any second premise you like, "Today is Monday and it is hot"; it is still as probable that tomorrow will be Tuesday as it is that today is Monday. But this fails to be the case when the step from premise to conclusion is inductive. Suppose I show you a small round disc with a head and tail which you readily identify as a half dollar. If I toss it, what is the chance that it will show a head? You say, "One-half; it is an even bet." But suppose I add that I bought this gimmick last week at Pete's Magic Shop for the purpose of this illustration: now what will you bet that if I toss it and it falls head up, it will not immediately turn itself over? The added information promptly diminishes the probability reasonably entertained on the ground of the first premise of your observation only. In particular instances it can happen, of course, that added information will *increase* the probability on antecedent grounds. But the point is that independent and added information may also *diminish* that antecedent probability: where the inference is deductive that can never happen; where the inference is inductive, it can and frequently does.*

---

* Where the inference is deductive and the premises are probable only, added information *may* decrease the antecedent probability of the conclusion if this added information is *not independent* of the antecedent premises. But in such a case this added information will decrease the antecedent probability of the conjoint statement of the antecedent premises also.

This seemingly small point has a consequence which is fundamentally important for the critical assessment of any inductively supported belief; the consequence, namely, that no inductive conclusion is well taken and justly credible unless the obligation to muster all the given and available evidence which is relevant to this conclusion has been met. If we can say, "This is all the evidence I command which bears upon this matter," and on this evidence, it is probable that A is the case, then A has just the warranted credibility so determined. But if pertinent evidence is ignored or suppressed, then any probability on the premises specified and utilized does not represent a warranted conclusion or a rationally justified belief.

We can observe this point quite simply by considering the nature of what we label "propaganda." Why is "propaganda" a derogatory name and what it designates untrustworthy and nonsignificant? Often, to be sure, because propaganda is based on premises which are falsehoods. But there could be an even more deceitful and more subtle kind of propaganda without resort to fiction in the premises. It would only be necessary to pick and choose amongst available and credible premises, always selecting those which are favorable to one's desired conclusion and sedulously avoiding any evidence which is unfavorable to it. By that method any ingenious logician could make out a case for almost any Alice-in-Wonderland conclusion. It is also just this method which the bigot unconsciously applies: he simply doesn't believe any evidence which is unfavorable to his bigoted conclusion; and if any such is put forward, he will argue it away by using this same method over again.

Indeed this principle of the required completeness of available and relevant evidence for the justified credibility of inductive conclusions, has a character which is plainly akin to the moral. It is unlike the textbook rules, which characteristically are formulations of routines to be followed, and has instead the character of a maxim. It calls upon us to be objective-minded, "reasonable," "fair," willing to give as much weight to what the opposition may put in evidence as to that which we advance ourselves. It demands that respect for facts as such prevail over any wish or subjective inclination. And—be it noted— this requirement for justified believing extends as widely as the inductive mode of substantiating belief; which means that it extends to most of our common knowledge and to all of natural science.* The following of textbook rules which represent prescribed or permissible routines for taking a step in inferring is not enough to assure the justification of inductive conclusions reached. A prevailing attitude of consideration, suggested by the words above, is further requisite. Not merely how we think, in the sense of proceeding one step after another in coming to a conclusion, but what we summon for con-

---

* Frequently the inferring of scientific conclusions is partly deductive and partly inductive. But in such cases, it is in point that any chain of inference is only as strong as its weakest link: if it be ninety-nine percent deductive and only one percent inductive, the warrant for the conclusion is still one hundred percent inductive. If at every step but one the conclusion is as certain as the premises, but for that one step the conclusion is established only with a probability m/n, then the conclusion of the whole train of inference has, on its total premises, only this probability m/n. On that account, it is appropriate to classify any whole chain of inference as inductive if any step of it is inductive. And even if any whole natural science should be reduced to the form of a deductive system, there would still be one inductive step unavoidably involved; that step, namely, in which anything in this deductive development should be applied to or affirmed as true of any natural phenomenon, empirically discovered.

sideration, is an essential point for right thinking and concluding. Otherwise, our thinking may be unexceptionably logical and yet be wholly specious in conclusion. No thinker or arguer is to be trusted unless he is first a man who conforms to this requirement of the objective-minded and reasonable, in a sense which is wider than the merely logical, and is prepared to give equal weight to whatever equally is fact and is relevant. Almost we may say that one who presents argument is worthy of confidence only if he be first a moral man, a man of integrity, prepared not only to tell the truth and nothing but the truth but also the whole truth as he knows it.

If we could follow out all the implications of this fact that our common knowledge and our justified beliefs prevailingly have no more than inductive warrant, and that justification of inductive conclusions requires that all known and relevant evidence be duly weighed, we might find that they run surprisingly far. It is for reasons akin to this, at least, that we presume, on the part of those who follow any scientific vocation, an acknowledged imperative so to include all available evidence, an attitude of respect for fact, and a sort of tacit professional oath never to subordinate the motive of objective truth-seeking to any subjective preference or inclination or any expediency or opportunistic consideration. We might also observe that this is a basic point for such "rights" as freedom of speech and assembly, freedom of investigation and communication, and one reason why suppression of the news and political censorship are social sins. Access to all available information is a common need, universal to those who have the capacity to determine their own believing and find it imperative to assess critically the manner of their thinking and concluding.

There is one other point on which observation of the basic character of the logically right and wrong can afford suggestions, if not carry implications, concerning right and wrong more generally and in other senses. It is a question whether the dictate of right always determines, or sometimes determines, or never determines just one unique decision or course of conduct, or whether there may be alternatives open to choice within the scope of what is right.

For that question, the answer with respect to the logically right, is that it depends on what the problem is. If it be the question, given this fact, must we accept, or must we repudiate, some other supposition, then plainly there can, in some cases, be one and only one right and logically dictated decision. If we are committed to belief '*P*' and '*P*' logically entails '*Q*,' then it is dictated that we believe '*Q*' and disbelieve the denial of it, if that question arises. Similarly, if '*P*' and '*Q*' be mutually implicative, logically equivalent, then belief or acceptance of either dictates acceptance of the other; and rejection of either requires rejection of both. If there were not such cases, logic would have no "force"; would carry no imperative at all.

But if the question be "Given '*P*,' or any set of premises, what shall I infer?" or "How shall I direct my course of thinking, in order to be right?" then the answer is different. Logic has sometimes been so written as to encourage the supposition that for premises of certain kinds there is just one conclusion which it will be right to draw—e.g., the syllogistic conclusion from premises of the pattern of traditional syllogisms. But that kind of supposition would, of course, be thoughtless. In the first place, logical paradigms are various, and may give different conclusions from the same premises. Whichever paradigm we choose to follow, our conclusion will be logically as right as if we choose another. There are even, amongst logical paradigms, some according to which an unlimited number of different conclusions are derivable from the same premises—and each and every one of them is right.

Indeed, as this should bring to our attention, if one who draws conclusions from given premises had no other and additional motivation beyond that of wishing to be logically justified, he would find himself in the predicament of Buridan's ass and not know which way to turn. For the direction of our thinking, some other and extralogical consideration—some dictate of purpose or interest—is always required, in addition to the logical critique.

Thus, so far as the evidence of logic goes, dictates of right sometimes require one unique resolution of a problem of believing or disbelieving. But with respect to the conduct and direction of our activity, they serve rather to divide possible termini of it into two classes, those which will be justified and those for which no justification is afforded; or into three, those specifically justified, those which are contraindicated as contravening what justification requires, and those which this particular dictate of the right neither requires nor disallows. Even within the logically right, then, we often have a choice. Whether right doing is like right thinking on this point, and whether this is characteristic of the right and wrong in general, are further questions. But as we already see, it cannot be the case that every dictate of right always gives a categorical and completely specific command, "Do this, and this only," leaving us no alternatives if we be right-minded. But also, as should be perfectly clear, any dictate of the right always forbids something.

In this brief survey of considerations affecting the validity of our thinking and the criticism of our concluding as right or wrong, we have perforce limited ourselves to certain topics only. But if the full subject of cogency in thinking and believing is too large for us here, we should in conclusion remark that fact. And it may be well to say two words concerning what has been omitted.

We have confined ourselves mainly to points which could be illustrated by reference to logic. Logic is only part of the critique of cogent thinking and belief. Its principles turn exclusively upon what is determinable by reference to consistency and inconsistency, and it might indeed be called the critique of consistency. That covers implicative relationships, since 'P' entails 'Q' just in case it would be inconsistent to believe or assert 'P' but disbelieve or deny 'Q.' But while inconsistency evidences that some falsity is involved, consistency by itself assures no truth and is never sufficient to justify any belief or asserted conclusion.

There might seem to be a difference of induction from deduction on this point, but that appearance is in fact misleading. No rule of induction ever warrants unqualifiedly a conclusion of the form, " 'Q' is rationally credible in degree m/n"; what it warrants is no more than that if the total pertinent evidence be 'P,' then 'Q' is credible in degree m/n. And if the rule applied is valid and really sufficient to the case, that *hypothetical* statement—strange as it may seem—is true a priori. Logical

criticism may determine that a conclusion or belief lacks justification, but except for what is assured a priori, it cannot by
itself determine any belief as positively justified. It cannot even
determine a (non–a priori) conclusion as justified since, as we
have observed, there is inference only where the conclusion is
affirmed or believed, and not asserted hypothetically only.

When we add to this the obvious fact that all natural science
and all empirical knowledge must eventually rest upon data
which are of the order of perceptual fact, we may observe, I
think, that nothing less than the full critique called theory of
knowledge could be adequate to the topic of justified concluding and believing. Or if the theory of knowledge, as traditionally pursued, fails in some part to accord with what is so
projected, at least we may recognize that there is, over and
above the logical critique of consistency, a further required
criticism of belief as justified which might be labeled the
"critique of cogency." However, if such separation is to be
made, this critique of cogency must either presume or include
the logical critique.

Right Doing

RIGHTNESS in concluding and believing is, perhaps, principally important to ourselves. Even if what we think should be finally significant only by affecting what we do, still the thinking is a separate activity, often carried out at some other time than the doing to which it is pertinent, and we have come to attach to truth and to the rightness of our thinking an importance distinct from that of any doing our beliefs may serve to guide. It is the rightness of our doing, however, with which other people are directly concerned. Whatever a man thinks, if his thinking it never moves him to do anything, or to refrain from doing, it will work no harm to others at least—nor produce any good. Ethics, being preeminently concerned with right and wrong in relation to others, is primarily directed upon the question of rightness in what we do. But ethics is not the only study so concerned: every art and every branch of technology also turns critical attention upon doing—as directed to those de-

sirable ends to which this art or technique is addressed. Also,
if few acts are entirely without effect upon others so that there
may be none which will be wholly exempt from the critique
of moral justice, it is likewise true that there are none at all
which are without effect upon the doer himself and are exempt from critical examination from the point of view of prudence. Prudential concern for one's own interest certainly is
rational, and its projected end, like the good of others for
which we are morally concerned, is something which will not
take care of itself without attention but perennially calls for
critical consideration of our contemplated acts. The modes of
the criticism of doing as right or wrong are, thus, various; and
ethics as usually pursued is only one of them.

It is also essential to remark that, while we may think without doing, and sometimes do without thinking, there is no
doing which is subject to criticism except as it reflects some
result of thinking or is amenable to taking thought, since it is
only behavior which is corrigible and self-governable for which
the doer is to be blamed or for which he merits any praise. As
has been previously noted, it is corrigible behavior alone—decidable doing—which will here be spoken of as "acting." Also
we shall apply the word "act" only when the thinking and deciding results in some physical bringing about. It is by reference to such eventuation in the outwardly observable physical
world that the determination or decision of doing is of a type
distinct from determination as to fact and decision of belief.
On the same ground also, even the decision to do must be distinguished from the doing and the act done. Though we cannot act, in the sense here taken, unless what is done is at least
amenable to decision, still it is clear that we can decide to act

without acting—as when we decide to do something later but indolently fail to carry out this intention when the time comes or recant our decision before the occasion for action arises.

Before we enter further upon these matters, however, let us pause briefly to observe the intimate and essential relations between thinking and believing on the one side and acting on the other which still obtains in spite of what has just been said. Though to think or even to decide is not to do, and where thinking leads to doing the two are still distinguishable, it is nevertheless dangerous to entertain a belief if we are not prepared to act upon it. Our convictions reached are, so to say, permanently stored up against any future and pertinent occasion—unless or until something happens to alter them. What we believe immediately affects what we are disposed to do, and becomes what we have called an active attitude. It is in result of this that our governable behavior may still be a matter of habitual response, and that occasions of action find us ready-prepared to act in ways which we approve, because we have on past occasions met this kind of problem and developed a well-settled way of acting in such cases. For example, we are held responsible, by ourselves and others, for our automobile driving; but we should never become good drivers if we continued to approach every intersection and every passing of another car as a problem to be decided, as we had to do at first. Believing that there is an intersection ahead, we follow a routine which originally represented decisions taken but has now become a matter of customary response—still good or not so good according to our previous and reflective decisions out of which this habit was allowed to develop. On any present occasion, this settled way of acting is still corrigible, and we are re-

sponsible for what we so do, not only because we can take
critical thought on this occasion and govern the doing deliberately, but also because the habitual mode of response is criticizable and correctible. But for any present and particular doing,
it is the active attitude which prevails unless we deliberately intervene upon it. And our convictions, representing past deliberations and decisions as to fact, are integral with such
active attitudes. Believing that honesty is the best policy, the
merchant is additionally disposed to giving customers the right
change. Believing that voting is essential to the preservation
of our democratic way of life, we are disposed to go to the
polls even though it interferes with recreation. If it were not
for the myriad well-settled facts of life stored away as convictions already reached, the processes of reality would come too
fast for us to do much of anything about them before the opportunity for action has passed. And also, they mostly go too
quickly for reconsideration of our ready-made convictions or
more than second thoughts which brush the surface of the
matter at hand. To question everything on every occasion of
its pertinence would be to do nothing; though to question
nothing would still be to do nothing responsibly and to be
comparatively ineffectual.

It is, indeed, plausible that the guidance of our conduct represents the vital function of belief, and that without the necessity of directing action we should debate no question but merely
behave as impinging stimuli and emotive feelings move us
to respond. There is the theory even—the "operational theory"
—that the meaning of any statement believed consists just in
the predictable consequences of doings or tests which we could
initiate and whose results, if they conform to such predictions,

will confirm the statement believed. But whether this conception of the intension of beliefs is fully adequate or not, at least it could hardly be denied that such consequences of action are involved in every belief concerning any matter of empirical fact. Every belief thus becomes a disposition to act—to act according as predicted consequences of so doing are desired or aimed at or are undesirable or ends which we repudiate. Also, any disposition to act deliberately implies some belief as to the consequences of it—if this action has any rationale. Any rightness of self-governed doing is hardly separable from the question of rightness of some believing which is implicated in this doing.

Every governed act begins as a mental process. There is some sense of alternative possibilities—at least the alternatives to do or not to do. These may be subject to reflection or even to long deliberation, but in any case there must be an expected sequel which figures in the decision to do. As we have seen, however, action may be decided upon but not committed; the decision and the commitment are distinct. The commitment is that inscrutable fiat of the will, the "oomph" of initiation, which terminates the mental part and is the bridge to the physical part of the act. Perhaps we should not call this distinctive phase of commitment inscrutable, since there is no other kind of mental item which so surely has our attention in the occurrence of it. But it is hardly describable—if any of us should stand in need of such description. Also, one committing of action appears to be the same as any other in its character as merely a committing: what distinguishes one such commitment from another is the difference of what we so commit ourselves to. What distinguishes the particular act and is specifiable as this particular commitment is simply the consequences of it, as expected. Perhaps we should not be able to distinguish the will-act itself from consequences which follow upon it if it were not that occasionally we take such initiative but what we expect fails to happen. For example, I will to raise my arm, but my sleeve is caught in the door and no arm-raising follows. Or my leg moves convulsively, but I know I didn't do it; there was no initiative with expectation of this; it just happened to me. It is this fiat or committing which is the doing itself, because until it is taken the action can be reconsidered, altered, or withheld; but after that the act is out of our hands and cannot be withdrawn. The rest of it simply occurs according to the laws of nature.

The first phase of the physical consequences of commitment is always some movement of the doer's body. We sometimes speak as if it were this bodily movement which is the act and is what we directly control. But, as just noted, our control of it is in fact less than perfect; it is merely an expected consequence of the commitment, our assurance of which is better than usually is the case for further consequences; and these further consequences are contingent upon it. However, this bodily doing can always—and correctly enough—be considered as the act done if we wish so to abstract it from anything further.

Considering it so, we may note that most such bodily doings are complex acts. They are divisible into some sequence: we can start them but halt them midway if we find them going wrong; and elements of this sequence are such as could be separately initiated, perhaps with time between and perhaps in a different order. Putting up a shelf or making a pie are such complex acts. But it would appear that there are other bodily acts, like swallowing or winking deliberately, which are elementary. Once we have initiated just that movement, we cannot halt it short of completion. These are of the all-or-none variety, and such an elementary act is wholly irrevocable once the initiative is taken. That the physiologist can analyze these also into some sequence of bodily events, does not affect the point: the understanding of winking as a physiological sequence does not enable one to halt half-way a wink which has been started.

We can tell how we do complex acts, and perhaps instruct others in the doing of them. But what can be so told is merely the parts and sequence of such doing. In the case of elementary acts, we cannot tell another or even tell ourselves how we do them; our "knowing how" they are performed is merely our awareness of ability to bring about this bodily movement at will. These facts constitute an additional reason for saying that the connection between the mental fact of the fiat of willing and the physical act done is inscrutable, and the sole content of any contemplation of an act considered lies in the thought of *consequences* of its commitment. We should remark, however, that even in the case of a complex act, one fiat of willing is often sufficient. After that, they may run themselves off chainwise and perhaps automatically—unless indeed we intervene upon their execution and, by a second initiative, halt them, or something external to our willing stops them.

Although the bodily doing, which is the first part of any physical bringing about, can always be considered as the act itself, it is seldom that we so think of an act done or to be done. Characteristically, what we speak of and think of in specifying an act in question is further consequences brought about, and most frequently with no thought or mention of the bodily movement in bringing them about. We so name or specify acts in various ways—typically, by referring to consequences of the commitment which, for one or another reason, are regarded as important. Oftentimes also, one and the same act may be variously designated, according to different interests we may have in it or different aspects of it to which we would call attention: for example, "He signed this paper," or "He contracted to sell a house"; "He placed his second finger on the stitching of the ball and released it with a leftward twist," or "He threw the strike that closed the inning." Sometimes we name an act according to consequences expected even though these may not follow: "He fired at the target"; "He went to see his brother." Again, we may designate the act by reference to actual consequences of the commitment even though they were not expected: "She swept the vase off the mantel with her dust-cloth." Sometimes we name an act in both of these last two ways at once; "He swerved to avoid the dog and wrecked his car." The one thing common to all designations of an act is that it will be consequences, actual or expected, which will be mentioned. There is nothing else we can recite by which an act meant can be distinguished from some other, except by reference to date, place, and doer, or other characteristics of the occasion on which it occurred. External circumstances, moreover, are never a part of the act, even though they may materially affect what will follow the commitment taken; first, because nothing antecedent to taking the commitment could be included in what is done, and second, because whatever the occasion and the nature of it, any corrigible act is one amongst some set of alternative ways of acting which the doer might have adopted on this occasion. An act is a difference which the commitment in question makes, or is expected to make, in the process of reality. That is basic and peculiar to our concept of an act; as an event merely, it might be otherwise described, but as an act it is an alteration of the future. It is always consequences, actual or expected, which are attributed to the doer as what he does or has done.

These considerations are important for the light which they may throw upon what it is which is assessed when an act done or contemplated is adjudged right or wrong. There is no content of an act but consequences of the commitment; there is nothing but consequences by which we could determine what act it is which we consider. When we criticize an act, what we criticize is the doer's commitment, because it is this commitment which is the doing of it. But our critical judgment of it can turn upon nothing but consequences, actual or expected, because it is by reference to consequences alone that one act could be distinguished and judged right from another which the doer might commit himself to do on this occasion which would be wrong. If there were no character of the consequences of act *A* by reason of which it is right or is wrong to bring them about, there could be no ground whatever on which act *A* is right or wrong.

Oftentimes, especially in ethics, intentions and consequences are contrasted. Sometimes theories of ethics are spoken of as if they were divisible into two classes, according as it is the intentions of acts or the consequences of them upon which moral rightness is conceived to turn. But if the distinction be so put, then it must be ill-expressed at least. What the intention of an act comprises is simply that total body of consequences which the doer expects in taking this commitment. Whether a particular result is one the doer desired or merely one he foresaw but was indifferent to, or even one he accepted regretfully for the sake of other results, it will in any case be correct to say that he brought it about intentionally if he expected it to happen as result of his commitment. If we need a narrower word for what is both expected and desired, we may use "purpose": the purpose of an act comprises the expected result or results for the sake of which it is adopted. Intentions and purposes do not, then, contrast with consequences; the pertinent distinction is merely between expected (intended) consequences and actual consequences which may coincide with or overlap or quite diverge from those expected. And intentions are right or wrong and criticizable only as the bringing about of what it is *intended to do* is right or wrong.

That manner of rightness which is attributable to an act if, and only if, it is rightly judged that its consequences are such as it will be right to bring about, may be called objective rightness. But let us note that the rightness of the judgment is a rightness of the kind which is ascribable to beliefs and judgments of fact. But a fact so judged is the property of the possible consequences of action—their being such as are right to bring about. What makes it right to bring about the consequences of an act, is one thing. What makes the judgment that a contemplated act is one having such consequences a right judgment, is another thing—the same sort of thing that makes any judgment of fact right; namely the weight of the evidence and correctness in drawing the conclusion from that evidence. It takes both these things to make an act objectively right.

That is, an act is objectively right if it is judged that its consequences are such as it will be right to bring about *and* that judgment is correct. What may stand in contrast to such objective rightness, and can be called subjective rightness, is the rightness of any act which the doer *thinks* will have consequences which it is right to bring about—whether his so thinking is a correct judgment or not. In other words, an act is subjectively right if the doer *thinks* it is *objectively* right, whether his so thinking is justified or not. One who *thinks* that what he does (the consequences he expects to bring about) is right to do, has "good intentions," though his judgment in so thinking may be unjustified and wrong. And if he has such good (right) intentions in doing, his act is subjectively right. But it is objectively right only if his intentions are right *and* his judgment in taking these intentions is right or correct judgment.

The distinction between objective rightness and subjective rightness is brought to our attention by contrasting ethical theories, some of which, like Kant's, emphasize intentions as what is determinative of the moral rightness of actions, and others, like utilitarianism, emphasize the kind of consequences which follow from these acts—e.g., the greatest good of the greatest number.

Let us note in passing that this distinction of subjective from objective rightness is not confined to moral judgment of acts but extends also to any mode in which acts can be judged right or wrong—to their prudential rightness or their technical rightness as well as to their character as just or unjust to others. The main points of this distinction are the same, whatever mode of right and wrong doing is in question. If we speak here mainly of ethics and moral rightness, what is said can be extended, in an obvious way, to the other modes of right and wrong doing as well.

One importance of this distinction of objectively right from subjectively right lies in the fact that, for any mode of the critique of doing, there are two kinds of problems upon which it may be directed. One is that of answering the question what it will be right to do in a given case; and the other is that of assigning praise and blame to doers, and perhaps of meting out reward or punishment for what is done. The first of these is the problem of any right-minded doer called upon to decide what he shall do. And it is a point to note that any doer who so deliberates his choice of action will hold himself responsible for *right thinking* as well as for conforming to what he thinks is right. Thus the problem of any deliberation of what it will be right or wrong to do is the question of the objective rightness of the doing.

But there is also a different kind of question about right and wrong doing; the question, namely, of praise and blame. How far, and on what grounds, shall we hold ourselves responsible if our well-intended act turns out badly? And what will others deserve, at our hands, when their intentions are good but their judgment of what acts should be done, in view of their consequences, is not so good? We have misgivings about both the practical effectiveness and the justice of punishing people for misjudging the results of what they do. And on other grounds, we have misgivings about penalizing others because they hold basically different convictions concerning the standards of right and wrong. The question what we shall blame and punish others for, or praise and reward them for, is a question *we* must settle because it is a question of *our own* conduct. On that question, sensible and civilized people decide that there is no justification for punishing honest errors of judgment. They are also likely to insist upon the privilege of each to do the right as it is given him to see the right, conceiving that this is something to be cherished and socially safeguarded. Somewhat similar considerations may affect our retrospective judgment of our own past doing, and of our past decisions as to right and wrong in doing, if later we recant them. We are all subject to errors of deliberation and conclusion, and the best that any of us can do is what he thinks is right at the time when decision of action is called for. Whoever does that is blameless. However, let us emphasize once more that whoever *thinks* his act right, thinks it *objectively* right; if he did not, then his doing it would not even be subjectively right. And if there were no objective rightness of action to be thought about, there would be no subjective rightness of it either.

Any adequate ethical theory must observe subjective rightness as well as objective rightness—if for no other reason, because retributive justice is a continuing social problem. But any ethics which fails to recognize the question of objective rightness also, or confuses the two, must be a fundamentally unsound theory. There is much which should be observed on just this point concerning various historical and contemporary theories of ethics, but we can note here only one way in which such inadequacy or confusion may arise.

In the first place, an ethical theory may be premised upon the conception that the primary concern of ethics is with the moral integrity of the doer and his final responsibility. The perfect judge will not blame us for errors we cannot help. The best we can do is to act from right intentions. Therefore, the rightness of our intentions should be our moral preoccupation; a rightly motivated act is morally right, and whatever a man thinks right is morally right for him to do. That is, it is possible to define the word "moral" by restricting it to the matter of intentions, and hence to the subjective rightness of action. And if this manner of interpreting the adjective "moral" is not explicit but introduced as something to be taken for granted, that merely makes it more difficult to untangle the inevitable complexities. There is, indeed, a highly important character of men which may be called their right-mindedness. This preparedness to do whatever they are convinced is right, is indeed the moral attitude. But is that the sole problem of ethics or even its major problem? Or is the main question justifying the study of our conduct the question what it is that right-minded men should do? If the only question which is material for right doing were "Do I think this contemplated action right to do; will my intention in doing it be good?" it would appear to be a rather simple matter to determine. Nobody can escape knowing what he *thinks* at the moment it is right to do. Indeed the subjective moralists have sometimes emphasized just that: "Every man can know his duty." But some of us have real trouble over that point—perhaps more trouble in being sure what, as right-minded men, we ought to do than in struggling against our original and perennial tendency to deliberate wrong doing. At least there is this other problem of the objectively right to do, and we are probably safe in thinking that this is not only the major moral problem but also the problem most students of ethics recognize as the first and foremost question they address.

Complete clarity on that point can, I think, go quite far toward unraveling this complex question of the objectively right to do, whether it is prudential rightness, or technical rightness, or justice—rightness toward others affected—which is to be assessed.

If there be any such problem of objective rightness, so that in a given situation there is that which a right-minded man should choose to do and other possible alternatives which he should avoid, then there must be some character of the consequences of these alternative actions open to the doer by reason of which one of them at least is right to do and others wrong. It must be some character of the consequences of action upon which this distinction of objectively right from objectively wrong will turn because, as we have seen, any consideration of an act has no content except the predicted consequences of it. It is only by reference to consequences that one act is distinguishable from another act. Let us designate the general character of the consequences of a contemplated act which stands as the criterion of their being right to bring about —that is, the character of ends it is right to aim at—by "G." We have not yet found out what this property is; and it will be a somewhat different character of the consequences according as the rightness to be judged is prudential or technical or that of social justice. Indeed, if we postpone that problem, just what character of consequences of the act it is which makes it right to bring them about by simply designating that character as "G," we are still not out of the woods, because of complications which we have not yet clearly faced. The problem faced in deliberating what it will be right to do has several parts. First, for each alternative of initiation open to us, there is the question what consequences will actually follow. Second, there is the question whether these consequences do or do not have the character G. Third, since we are obliged to predict these consequences and to assess predictively their character as G or not-G, there is the question what degree of assurance of our predictive judgment, on both points, will be cognitively warranted. We might, if we chose, designate an act as objectively right if and only if the total of its *actual* consequences *actually* has the character G. But so to do would make it impossible to determine anything as thus objectively right, and this would be a useless way of using the designation. Nobody ever knows all the consequences of anything he does. And it is at least doubtful whether anyone could be completely certain in advance that even the foreseen consequences of the act have such a character as G, or indeed any particular character we might choose to mention. The best one can hope for is to *judge correctly,* on the basis of whatever evidence is open to him, what consequences which are important will follow upon any contemplated initiative of his and to judge correctly, on the available evidence, whether or how far these anticipated consequences will have the desiderated character G. Both these matters, like all empirical facts we are obliged to judge, will lack any one hundred percent certainty. Some may come so close to it, on evidence at hand, as to be "practically certain." But where it is consequences of our doing which are in question, it is quite clear that much of what we shall be called upon to judge can only be determined with some degree of probability.

What we must make judgment *of,* in the case of deliberate action, is of course a matter of one hundred percent fact, even though fact about the future—what consequences actually

would ensue upon a way of acting considered and what character these consequences would actually have. But the most
that any doer can do is to determine his conclusions on both
points according to the available evidence; to reach conclusions
which, whether *true* of future facts or not, are *justified judgments*. Especially since any matter of right and wrong is
always a question of justification, and correctness within the
possible, the appropriate and useful way of using the phrase
"objectively right" of deliberate acts, will be to say that an act
is objectively right if and only if, in the circumstances and on
all the pertinent evidence available to the doer, it is that alternative of action which affords the highest probability of realizing
consequences having that character we have designated as
"G." The objectivity of objective rightness, so taken, consists
in the fact that a probability-judgment from given evidence is
right or wrong in the same sense as any other inference; it is
not a matter of opinion or in any other sense subjective, but a
matter of logical fact. One who judges such a fact is either
right or wrong according as the evidence justifies this probability-conclusion or fails to justify it; and no two incompatible conclusions from the same evidence could both be right.
On the same terms, an act would be subjectively right if the
doer be convinced (whether correctly or incorrectly) that his
act has this character of objective rightness.* The point of

* As already suggested, it could also be subjectively right, though not
objectively right, if the doer honestly mistakes the criterion (G) by
reference to which the consequences of an act are to be weighed in
judging what it is right to bring about.

The two phrases "objectively right" and "subjectively right" have
been variously used by ethical theorists; the distinction as here made
does not quite coincide with any such previous usage. I can only hope

difference between objective rightness and subjective rightness is, thus, that an act is subjectively right if it conforms to the doer's conviction concerning what consequences are likely to follow and their having that character which marks them as justified to bring about. But an act is objectively right only if this conviction is a cognitively correct judgment—a probability-conclusion correctly drawn from the available evidence.

As has already occurred to you, perhaps this mysterious property G which is the distinctive feature of consequences which may justify an action, is simply *good*. Let me say at once that I think that to take it so would be, at this stage, both unclear and an oversimplification. But let us make that oversimple assumption, for the moment, in order to round out a sort of first approximation to the full answer concerning the objective rightness of action. An act, then, is objectively right to do just in case, on the evidence available to the doer, it is that alternative of action which affords the (correctly judged) highest probability of good results. The goodness in question will be goodness for the doer himself if it is prudential rightness which is to be determined. Technically right action will be similarly determined by reference to technical excellence. And action which is right in the sense of moral justice, will be similarly judged—let us assume for the moment—by reference to the conjoint good of all whom this action in question will affect.

So taking it, we may resolve, provisionally, the last point of a major sort which need be mentioned. Goodness has degrees, and probability has degrees. How should we determine objective rightness where conjectured consequences of the act would

that the discussion itself will justify the manner in which it is here drawn.

be good in high degree but the probability of their being realized is not large? A different alternative of action would—let
us say—afford a *larger* probability of a *lesser* goodness in the
consequences. The general principle here would, of course, be
the obvious one; a near certainty of half a loaf is better than
one chance out of five of getting a whole one. That kind of
answer, too, may be oversimple, but at least it suggests that this
last point is one which also can be resolved, allowing questions
of what it is right to do to have a correct and objectively determinable answer, independent of what anyone may think about
them or anybody's emotive feelings or other subjectivity of
opinion or inclination.

However, "good" is a word of many meanings, and even
provisional correctness of the provisionally suggested answers
above will call for further examination of the modes in which
goodness is assessed and any relation of these modes to corre-
sponding modes of the right. We shall proceed to that topic in
the next chapter.

The Right and the Good

ANTECEDENTLY to any inquiry, it is obvious that there must be some essential connection between the right and the good. No act would be called right if nothing but bad results could be expected from it; and to condemn as wrong an act which could not possibly lead to anything but good would surely be a puritanical conception which we should reject. Also, if there were nothing good or bad which could come about, and life were in no wise subject to enjoyment or to suffering, it seems plain that the distinction of right and wrong would disappear along with that of good and bad. Any ethical theory, though its main business is delimitation of the morally right, must also deal with the subject of the good—perhaps under title of the *summum bonum*—and with this question of the manner in which what is right depends on what is good.

However, before the right and the good are to be related they must first be distinguished, and the distinction of them is at least as difficult as finding precisely the essential connection between the two.

In the broad, the requirement of this distinction may be plain enough. The achievement of the good is desirable but conformity to the right is imperative. And second, nothing is strictly right or wrong except some possible activity or the manner of it, whereas in an equally strict sense anything under the sun may be good or bad. But what it signifies to speak of the imperative, is none too clear. And the fact that good and bad are attributable to things of diverse categories includes the fact that, amongst other things, actions and decisions may be good or bad as well as right or wrong. Add to this the consideration that, by the general metonymy affecting the use of language, terms applied originally and strictly to one class of things may come to be extended to whatever else is commonly associated with things of that class, and the difficulties of marking off the right from the good, the wrong from the bad, become extreme.

It does not help in this connection, but hinders, that ethicists frequently speak as if moral rightness were the only category of the right, thus obscuring the question whether the essential relation we must seek is one which holds between moral rightness and moral (or social) good, or between moral rightness and the good at large, or between the right in general and the good in general. Also it does not help, but hinders, that those who concern themselves with value-theory sometimes take value as comprehending both the good and the right, thus construing judgments of the right as one type of valuations and making the term "value" significant of the normative in general.

Let us do no more violence to idiom than is necessary, but let us first seek out those *root* senses of "right" and of "good" in terms of which the distinction of these may become clear. When we have done that, perhaps we can also find out what connects the two.

As we have seen, "right" and "wrong" can only be applied to acts by specifying consequences of the commitment; and in result we can hardly say that an act is right without implying that predictable consequences of it are right to bring about. But let us note that when we say that certain consequences of action are "right to bring about" or "wrong to bring about," the rightness or wrongness is attributed to the act which brings them about, and not to the consequences as happenings or states of affairs apart from relation to a commitment of doing. What we should observe, in this connection, is the syntactic ambiguity of statements of the form, "A is right to bring about": the adjective "right" here modifies the infinitive "to bring about," though it may appear to modify the subject "A." Mistake over this small point of idiomatic usage could obscure a most important problem of ethics.

For example, if we give directions to a stranger by telling him, "Cedar Street will be right for you to take," we do not predicate any property of rightness to Cedar Street: the rightness is attributed to his choice of it; to his decision or act of taking it. In less idiomatic but more precise English; "To take Cedar Street will be right for you" or "Your taking Cedar Street will be right." This idiom is not confined to instances in which it is rightness or wrongness which is attributed. When, for example, the cook says, "Sponge cake is hard to make," the hardness is attributed to the making, not to the sponge cake—though the cake may be hard too, in a different sense. What she means is, "To make sponge cake is hard"; "Making sponge cake is hard."

The similar remark applies wherever consequences of action, or expected consequences, appear to be spoken of as right or wrong: "That consequence is right to bring about" means, "It is right to bring about that consequence"; "The bringing about of that consequence is right." It is the decision to aim at these consequences, or the act of bringing them about, which will be right or wrong; there is no implication that the consequences themselves have any property of rightness or wrongness, just as there is no implication that a sponge cake which is hard to make will be a hard sponge cake.

The importance of these observations is not so much avoidance of the supposition that the consequences of action have, in themselves and apart from any decision or commitment, a property correctly called their rightness or their wrongness— we should hardly fall into that confusion more than momentarily. What is important is that we should not overlook the fact, already pointed out, that there must indeed be *some* character of the predictable consequences of action by reason of which the commitment to bring about these consequences will be a right, or a wrong, commitment to take. Only so could a wholly right-minded doer find out, in a given situation, what alternative of action will be right for him to take, and distinguish this alternative from others which would be wrong. He must find this distinction by reference to some character of the consequences of the alternative commitments open to him. Moreover, this property of the expected consequences, by reason of which one act will be right and another wrong, must be one which the consequences have independently of any doer's choosing to bring them about; otherwise the choice would be impossible.

Solution of the central problem of ethics requires us to determine what character of the consequences of action it is by reference to which one act will be right and another wrong. Our tentative suggestion is that this distinguishing property of the consequences is their goodness or their badness. The present point is merely that it could not be their rightness or wrongness: results of action, taken by themselves, could not be either right or wrong; they *could* have, and *do* have, the property of goodness or badness independently of any doer's decision or commitment to bring them about.

Perhaps it will still be objected that there is another sense in which right and wrong may be applied to consequences, or even to things which are not consequences of any commitment at all. Without reference to any doer or to any particular act or activity, we may still call something right or wrong. To take an extreme example, an artist in search of a subject may see the morning light falling on some craggy hillside and say, "That is exactly right." But surely this pattern of form and color is such as nobody could be responsible for, or either praised or blamed for. What we here meet is a similar metonymy of language which can cause confusion. The intention of this usage is to be explained, is it not, by the thought that this landscape is such as an artist would be artistically justified in choosing to portray. Strictly, the rightness is attributable to some hypothetical choosing or the pictorializing of this subject. Apart from such implicit reference to a possible decision or commitment of doing, what the artist sees may properly be called good but improperly called right.

The difficulties of avoiding such merely syntactic anomalies and metonymous usages is even greater when we come to "good" and "bad." Not only must we allow for that essential connection of right with good and wrong with bad which has been presumed, but we must observe that acts themselves, like every other kind of things, may be good or bad—in addition to and in a different sense from that in which acts are right or wrong. It is also another point of difficulty that the idiomatic language of morals is quite thoroughly confusing. We customarily speak of moral goodness when what we really mean is moral rightness; of morally good men when we should, in order to be precise, speak of righteous or upright men; and of morally good and morally bad acts when what we mean is morally right or morally wrong acts. Strictly there is no such thing as moral goodness or moral badness: moral distinctions apply only to doers, who are right-minded and upright or the opposite, and to their deeds or their intentions, which are right or wrong.

The sense in which acts, and men as doers of them, are strictly to be called good, is a quite different one: the sense, namely, of being useful; of contributing or being able to contribute to some desirable end. And in that sense, a man may be a good man—a good team member, for example, or a handy chap to have around—even if he is not righteous or even upright. If the combination of a safe has been lost, a skilled safe-robber may be a good man to send for. Similarly, an act may be strictly good in the sense of furthering some end or purpose. And in that sense something unjustified to do may still be good, as when we say, "That was quite the wrong thing to do, but it is good (fortunate) that he did it." Normally, of course, an act which is strictly right, will also be strictly good; it will further some desirable end. But as we have just seen, it does not have to be right in order to be good; and the remaining question is whether it has to be good in order to be right. The answer to that question also is "No." An act deliberately directed to a rightly chosen end is subjectively right in any case, whether it does any good or not. And an act may also be objectively right even though it does no good; it may fail of any good result on account of circumstances nobody could foresee, and in that case will still have been wholly justified to decide upon, both cognitively and in every other sense.

These matters, as well as others which are involved, could hardly become clear without observation of at least some of the great variety of modes in which goodness and badness are assessed. But on this point we must be as brief as possible. Considerations supporting the conclusions stated, or defending the classifications made and utilized, may be omitted.*

The root of goodness and badness in life lies in the fact that humans, like other animals, enjoy and suffer and find the quality of experience as it comes to them gratifying or grievous. And the root senses of "good" and "bad," "value" and "disvalue," reflect that fact. There is indeed nothing which is desirable or undesirable for its own sake and entirely without reference to anything beyond itself except that quality of passages of experience by which he who experiences them finds them satisfying and such as he would prolong, or dissatisfying and such as he would terminate or avoid. Using the adjective "intrinsic" in this sense of "for its own sake," the only kind of thing thus intrinsically good or bad is experience itself or the content of it. But humans, if not other creatures as well, learn to identify objects and happenings in the external world as causative agen-

---

* Such considerations, so far as I am able to provide them, have been set forth in Book III of *An Analysis of Knowledge and Valuation* (La Salle, Ill., Open Court Publishing Company, 1946).

cies, productive of these qualities of our experience. And "good" and "bad" and other value-terms are extended to those objective things and events and to those characters of them which we identify as causing such good or bad experience. In consequence, the generic value-terms, as well as others which are more specific, come to have two distinguishable senses: (1) as applying to experience directly and signifying the gratifying or grievous quality of it, and (2) as applied to objective things of various kinds and signifying potentialities of them for producing or conducing to experiences which have these qualities. These two senses require to be distinguished because to say that an *experience* is good or pleasing means one thing, and to say that an *object* is good or is pleasing means something different. For one point, the experience is transitory but the object is more or less enduring and may affect experience again. And for another, every experience is personal and private, but an object may affect the experience of many persons. To say that an experience which pleases is a pleasing experience, is a tautology. But to say that an object which pleases is a pleasing object, is not a tautology; that same object may fail to please us on another occasion, and may displease other persons. To say that an object is pleasing means—if the statement is a clear one—that this object is characteristically capable of producing pleasure in the experience of those who may be affected by it.

Such duality of reference—to experience and the quality of it, or to objects as causing experience of that quality—is one ambiguity which affects value-terms, and it is to be dispelled by asking, "What are you talking about?" When one stands in front of a picture and says, "Good," is he talking about his experience of the moment or is he talking about the picture? If he is talking about his experience, then he is reporting an immediate quality of it, about which he could hardly be mistaken. But if he is talking about the picture, then this quality of his experience may be *evidence* that this is a good picture, but it doesn't prove it. For proof, one would better wait and see whether he still finds the picture pleasing after it has hung on his wall for a while, or ask other persons whether they find it pleasing, or offer it for sale and see what someone will pay for it.

However, this particular ambiguity of value-terms is not one which can be dispelled by deciding in favor of one of these two modes of their meaning and discarding the other. Both are required if we are to make any sense of valuations at all. We might be inclined to disregard direct value-findings in transitory experience as merely subjective and trivial. But if so, then we should remind ourselves that, though the experience is transitory, the occurrence of it with just this value-quality is a fact—is indeed that kind of fact in the absence of which there would be no meaningful distinction of good and bad at all. When we ascribe a value to the picture or to any other presentable object we are attributing to it an objective quality by reason of which it is capable of giving rise to just this kind of experience, on the part of ourselves or of others.

Moreover, the case is different if it is a future and predictable experience of which we speak instead of one whose quality is indubitable because we presently have it. And questions of values and disvalues to be found in future or possible experience, represent a most important type. They are sure to be involved in the deliberation of any action. It is only as we are able to make such predictions that we can so govern action as to serve our future happiness and avoid unhappiness. And without some control over the value-quality of one's future living, any capacity to affect the future in other respects would be a matter of indifference. Let us also note that, unlike predictions of future facts about objects and the external world, these predictions as to our own future experience can be decisively verified by the predicted experience when it comes.

We also make judgments concerning the value-qualities of experiences we predict or regard as possible for others. And let us not be misled by the obvious dubieties affecting our apprehension of the experience of other persons into any belittlement of the possibility and practical importance of such judgments. It is only by some assurance in judgments of that sort that we can do anybody else any good—or any harm. For the social animal, considerable accuracy in judging the satisfaction or dissatisfaction which his actions may cause to others, is essential for keeping out of trouble, to say nothing of making friends and influencing people.

It is also of first importance to observe that ascription to experience of a value or disvalue which resides in the immediate quality of it as gratifying or grievous, does not represent the only mode in which values are attributable to experience. Passages of experience not only have such directly found goodness or badness within their own boundaries; they also make their contribution to that life on the whole in which they are ingredient. To be sure, a good life could not be constituted exclusively of grievous moments; nor could one made up of gratifying experiences only, be a bad one to live. But for a variety of reasons, which, being familiar, need not be recited here, an immediately dissatisfying experience may be salutary and contribute more to the goodness of a life than any alternative to it, while an immediate gratification on a specific occasion may be notably prejudicial to the over-all goodness of future living.

Let us also note that although there is nothing in a conscious life except those passages of experience which make it up, nevertheless this statement itself is a near-falsification because a life as lived is not the sum of its separate moments. The goodness or badness of a life on the whole is not to be found, as Bentham thought, by adding up the transient gratifications of it and subtracting the sum of its griefs. Life is experienced in some part, and pervasively, whole-wise or *Gestalt*-wise, much as we hear a symphony which is being played and not merely as a succession of notes or chords one after the other. Also, life—especially life as active—is not a summation but consummatory. To eat one's peck of dirt in youth and so achieve a life ambition is quite different from spending one's youthful energies in exuberant enjoyment and finding the peck of dirt left for middle-age. Once again, life is like heard music; not only the constituent passages but the order and progression of them make a difference to the quality of it on the whole.

Let us call the value assignable to any transitory experience not—or not merely—by reason of the quality it immediately presents but on account of its contribution to some larger whole of experience, or to life altogether, the *contributory* value of it. And the goodness of life, or of a life, on the whole, whether it be our own life we speak of or that of another, surely should be called the *final* good; it represents the *summum bonum*.

By contrast to these values—or these modes of valuing—in which the value-characteristics are ascribed to experience itself, any value attributable to any object or event or other external thing can be extrinsic only. It is good that good objects exist, in order that we may derive experienced good from them, but if no one could ever possess or enjoy them they would still be worthless. The goodness of any good object is simply what it may or might contribute to some conscious life; and this value of the object is not for its own sake but for the sake of such gratifying experience it may afford. There is, however, an important distinction amongst the values so ascribable to objects, according as the satisfaction to which they may give rise is one to be found in the presence of the object itself and as a direct effect of it, or is one to be found in the presence of some other thing or things whose production or availability to us this object in question facilitates. Let us call those values which objects have by their capacity to contribute directly to human life by their presence, *inherent* values. And let us call the mere usefulness of an object for the production of something else which is desirable, an *instrumental* value of it. An art-object, for example, has inherent value: it conduces to a satisfaction to be found in the presence of it. All aesthetic values are such inherent values. By contrast, the painter's brushes and the canvas he uses typically have a value which is instrumental only and not inherent. The value of tools in general is characteristically of this instrumental sort; we value them for what they lead to or make possible and otherwise would find no satisfaction in having them. However, we should observe, of course, that many things have both some inherent value and some instrumental value: they afford some direct satisfaction by their presence and they also serve some further purpose.

Furthermore, it is a law of life—one which is most important and a matter for congratulation—that whatever is habitually associated with the directly gratifying tends to become itself gratifying. This is one side of the fact which psychologists call conditioning, though perhaps the psychologists are unwarrantedly prone to think of it as something which external circumstances and other people do to us and to deemphasize the fact that creatures who govern their own activities in some measure also take a hand in conditioning themselves. That point—that we ourselves determine, in some part, that in which our values will be found—is of much importance in connection with right doing and for the characteristic goodness of a moral life. The satisfactions so findable in self-determined activity, directed in accord with our convictions of the right, are ego-involved and go deep, even if they should be less intense than others. Such goods of integrity, as we may call them, are those of self-realization, and the value of them as contributory to a life to be found good in the living of it, can be preeminent.

Another basic distinction amongst values, and one likewise fundamental for ethics, is that which lies between the *personal* values and impersonal or *social* values. Personal values—value to me, value to you, value to John Doe—are separately assessed by reason of the personal differences and differences in personal circumstances affecting the satisfactions we may derive from things and the usefulness of them to us. But lest we should be misled into supposing that such personal values are relative or subjective merely, let us observe two facts about them: first, that the character of anything by reason of which it is gratifying—as, for example, good music is gratifying to people of musical sensitivity but not to those who are tone-deaf—is just as much an objective property of the thing as the color of it or the rate of vibration it gives off when struck. Second, and even more important, the social values are improperly conceived if it be supposed that they are ascribable only to things which are directly gratifying to everybody. Economic value, for example, will be recognized as one important type of impersonal and objective value attaching to things. But the fact that few of us would find any personal use for a silo full of chopped cornstalks does not deprive it of impersonal and objective value. The contents of the silo has a social value and is economically desirable. It is socially gratifying that the farmer should have it because of a relation between him and the rest of us; his having it results in more, and hence cheaper, milk in the market. Social value is obviously an intricate subject, but broadly speaking we may say that the social values of things are values which they have for *some* of us, at least, in ways which are not subversive of but may conduce to the interest in a good life for all of us together. Social value is definitely not confined to those things which are useful or gratifying to all of us alike. Tendency to that misconception is one root fallacy of totalitarianism and the regimented society. What is useful to or gratifies any member of a society and brings no harm or distress to any other, has by that fact some measure of impersonal and social value. That is a root thesis of Western civilization, predicated upon respect for each and every individual and his possible achievement of a good life. And that thesis, as I shall hope to indicate, represents no merely emotive inclination to benevolence, perhaps more prevalent in the materially better circumstanced Western societies, but reflects a categorical imperative.

And now let us return to questions which more specifically concern the essential relation or relations between the good or valuable and what it is right to do. If our hasty review of the different required senses of "good" or "value" has any relevant significance, then it will at least indicate the necessity, when any question of relation between the good and the right is raised, of asking first, "Good in what sense; what kind of goodness?" and perhaps also, "Right in what sense; what kind of rightness?"

Any attempt to determine right action directly and simply in terms of the goodness of its results—or the doer's expectation of good results, or his *justified* prediction of goodness in the results—will unavoidably encounter problems of a different sort, including most obviously the question, "Personal goodness to the doer himself, or social good to all who are affected?" And that kind of question, what species of goodness or manner of its assessment is in point, is itself a basic issue of right doing and one over which moralists have disagreed. The egoist answers that question in one way, the social utilitarian in another; and whichever of them is right—if either—this issue itself cannot be settled by appeal to the criterion of maximum goodness to be achieved. So to determine it would be to give the case to the utilitarians on a *petitio principii*. If we recognize that it is morally required to give precedence to justice over prudence when the two conflict, that still leaves the question, "But what is justice and what are its dictates?" There is, for example, that outstanding kind of objection to utilitarianism: "But is it *just* to sacrifice an unwilling victim to save the nation from disaster?" The question whether whatever will maximize the social good is forthwith just, is still a moral issue. If there were no other kind of determinant of what it is right to do than merely the preponderant goodness of total results, that issue of justice not only would be already answered, it would be gratuitous to raise it, since the correct answer would be merely tautological. But we hardly could admit that this question about justice is thus gratuitous. Consonantly, we cannot accept any utilitarian account which would make it such, as sufficient on the point raised.

Even with respect to the simpler question of the prudentially justified to do—separating that from all others—there are also issues of this sort. For example, the question what manner of weighing the goodness of results to the doer determines the prudent choice of action, has received at least three different answers in the history of ethics. The Cynics repudiate prudence altogether as having no sanction; not maximum goodness to oneself but the goodness immediately to be grasped determines the justified thing to do—so far as any choice of action is better justified than another. Bentham, who recognizes the prudential sanction and indeed regards it as the only final sanction of any act as right, nevertheless disagrees with most of us as to that manner of weighing consequences which correctly determines the prudential choice. Over and above the intensity, duration, and probability of satisfying or dissatisfying consequences (pleasure or pain, in his terms), he would give weight to the "propinquity or remoteness" of them. That is, he thinks that a nearer good can outweigh an otherwise greater good if the latter be sufficiently further in the future.* Sidgwick, by contrast (like

* There is some question whether this is merely an inadvertence on Bentham's part, and he is influenced by the consideration that more remote consequences are, generally speaking, less certain to be realized. But he cites this dimension of propinquity or remoteness separately from probability.

most of the rest of us), considers that the time when a good or bad consequence of action is to be expected should make no difference for the weighing of it. The prudential aim, we probably shall agree, is the maximization of the balance of good over bad to be realized by the doer in result; to weigh a nearer good more heavily than a distant one is the common failure of those who are not, or not sufficiently, prudent. Certainly that mode of assessment prejudices realization of the maximum possible goodness in a whole life. But the issue cannot be supposed settled by a correct definition of "prudence," any more than the question of sacrificing individual good to the social welfare is decidable by a definition of "justice": the labels we attach to actions do not affect the justification of them.

Such issues as those mentioned could be settled if we had a rule or valid directive of prudential decisions, a rule of justice, and a rule for weighing prudence and justice one against the other. And without something operative in the manner of a rule or principle, no weighing of good or bad consequences of action will determine any act as right or wrong in any sense—unless, as is altogether unlikely, we can determine the act as having *no* bad consequences, or none which are good.

On the other hand, no rule, by itself, can forthwith determine any act as right or wrong to do except as the specification of the act considered includes circumstances by reason of which the rule is pertinent. Indeed, for a rule to apply to an act, it will be necessary both that the rule be, explicitly or implicitly, such as will indicate its relevance to cases of a certain kind, and that the act be so understood as to make clear that the rule applies. The rule and the act must, so to say, have a term in common, like a major and a minor premise, in order that a conclusion as to rightness of the act, under this rule, should be derivable.

We have observed, however, that there hardly could be a rightness or wrongness of any species which attaches to any act, without reference to some mode of goodness or badness with which consequences of the act, as predicted, will be affected. Where there should be no goodness or badness involved, there could be no question of what it is right or wrong to bring about; and the question what it is which is to be brought about is the question what act it is which is under consideration. It would appear then, prima facie, that, explicitly or implicitly, some import of goodness or badness represents the middle term which is common to any rule of right doing and any case to be decided under that rule. The Golden Rule, for example, makes no explicit mention of good or bad but, by setting as the criterion what we should wish to realize at the hands of another, it plainly implies goodness of the consequences to other individuals as essential to rightness of our acts affecting them.

It takes two things, then, to determine the rightness of action: a rule or directive of right doing, or something operative in the manner of a rule, and a judgment of goodness to be found in the consequences of the act in question. Characteristically, we should think of the judgment of good consequences as determining the sanction of this act by the rule, and of the rule itself as sanctioning acts of this class; as a general directive extending to this case.

Observation that it takes both these things to constitute an act right is, I think, often overlooked, and one or the other of them may be cited as if it alone were a sufficient ground of such rightness. Possibly that helps to explain the opposition between those who emphasize goodness and consequences and those who emphasize conformity to principles and moral perfection. Insofar as this is the explanation of such opposition, we should observe that the opposition itself is a mistake: each of these emphases represents a half-truth which needs the other as its supplement. The *proximate* determination of an act as right will be by way of assessment of its consequences as good. But that is the minor premise of the moral syllogism; the major premise is some valid rule or principle conveying the general sanction of acts of this class and having such consequences. Either one of the two being given or presumed, it is the other which "makes the act right to do," but without presumption of the other, neither will be sufficient to determine rightness in a particular instance.

However, if it is the imperativeness of any act which is in question, or if it is the ground of any species of rightness which engages us, then we shall look to the rule or principle; it is the rule which carries the sense of a directive; and what consequences an act has, or what kind of consequences, is simply a matter of empirical fact. Also, it is the rule which, by its generality, may have that kind of significance normally looked for in matters of "explanation" or questions of "ground." For the same reason, we seek the general and high-level kind of rules commonly connoted by the word "principle," rather than "rules of thumb," "maxims," or rules themselves derivative from or presupposing others which are more fundamental.

Even such high-level rules, extending to some whole category of the right, may still be quite diverse from one another in the nature of the directives which they convey. Also, there is that most important difference of all: some are "right rules," "really rules," really binding in some connection or in general, and some are merely precepts or directives mistakenly accepted or even wrongly and perversely adopted or promulgated. Some general directives are valid and some which may be proposed are not. The question so raised, of what distinguishes a rule or principle as valid and itself right, is, of course, the deepest-going and the most difficult of all questions concerning right and wrong.

The Rational Imperatives

FROM THE START of these brief investigations we have had it in mind, as one desideratum, to approach the subject of ethics. In so short a study we could not hope, of course, to touch upon anything beyond what is most fundamental for the morally right or even to include more than suggestion of the fundamentals. Ethics is a most complex subject, and any attempt to reduce it to simple terms would be ill-judged and doomed to failure. What we have hoped is that it might illuminate problems of the moral to compare this category of the right with others and with the right in general.

What we seem to find is that the right at large concerns activities which are corrigible and determinable by decision, and hence are subject to deliberation and to critical assessment. In its connotation of the deliberate and deliberable, the right exhibits essential connection with the peculiarly human character of our mentality as cognitive and reflective. No manner of behavior wholly untouched by thinking could be right or wrong; and it is only such thinking as is bent upon the determination of fact and has the intent of some objective reference which is subject to normative assessment.

Since it is only such doing as is amenable to deliberation which could be right or wrong, criticized doing presumes thinking which may itself be criticized, as well as criticism of that which is brought about in the light of such thinking. For doing to be right in the fullest sense—objectively right, as we have called it—the thinking which underlies it must be consistent and cogent; characterized by that objectivity and integrity which summons all pertinent evidence and gives all items their due weight in conclusions drawn, as well as conforming to logical requirements.

What is additionally involved in the criticism and the justification of doing, beyond rightness of the thinking in the light of which it is determined, lies in the fact that doing alters the world about us and has consequences, in a sense in which thinking, if it could be completely separated from any physical bringing about, would have no consequences but leave the external world as it found it and as it will otherwise become. And what has import of the criticizable in such doing concerns the consequences of it as good or bad. If it were not for the qualities of good and bad in life and our possible effect upon them, there would be no point in doing, and it is at least doubtful that there would be any point in objective thinking. Broadly and loosely speaking, to do that the consequences of which are justifiably expected to be good rather than bad, is the objectively right way to act; and doing that which justified belief would indicate to have bad consequences rather than good, is the objectively wrong way to act. But the right and wrong in action are not determinable, simply and directly, by reference to good or bad consequences, because of the fact—amongst others—that what is justifiably believed may still be false, and what is justifiably disbelieved may still be true.

It is further pertinent to right and wrong that it is only *ways* of thinking and of doing which we can learn how to direct or govern, since it is only what characterizes more than one instance of activity which can be learned, or directed by any manner of knowing how. Activity is directable only as it answers to some generality, represents some mode, and hence is amenable to some formulatable rule of procedure. Consonantly all activities, in being criticizable only as governable modes of our self-direction, are likewise criticizable by reference to formulatable directives. It is by reference to such implicit or explicit directives of doing—directives themselves determined with included reference to the good or bad results of conforming to them—that right and wrong in doing are finally determinable.

The main modes in which the right or wrong of doing is assessed are the technical, the prudential, and that of justice as adjudged in the light of predictable consequences to all who are affected.

The technical critiques are the simplest, since they assume some species of desirable results, and presume this general desirability of them as antecedently determined fact. Thus a technical critique is critical of activity only in its relation to some such class of ends assumed as justifying that which will lead to realization of them. Its directives are the product of past experience indicating those modes of governing the technical activity which will, most reliably, produce such desirable, as against undesirable, results. The rightness of the directives themselves derives from this presumed goodness of the results and the reliability of achieving such results by following these directives, or from the unjustified character of expecting such good results if they are not heeded. Any imperativeness attaching to the technical rules is a matter of "if, as, and when"—if, as, and when the presumption that activity directed to the technical end is an otherwise justified decision of doing or choice of what to do. Kant called them hypothetical imperatives; and the sense in which that is appropriate will be evident.

However, as we noticed earlier, there is a kind of qualification to be observed here, especially if the term "technical" be extended to practice of the arts and professions. Such practice affects ends which are wider than the technical and is, so far forth, subject to criticism on moral grounds rather than on grounds relating to technical excellence or shortcoming. It is so that medical ethics is well-named; and the similar point is to be observed in the code governing the relation of the attorney to his clients, to his professional brethren, and to the courts. Such moral precepts as are peculiarly pertinent to the practice of a vocation may be collated with the critique of it as technically right or wrong but, strictly, they do not represent a part of the technical critique.

The prudential critique and the rules of prudence could be dealt with in the same manner as the technical: regardless of further considerations, one could surely say that determination of action by directives conformity to which will, as men have learned, reliably conduce to achievement of the doer's own good, is imperative if, as, and when the direction of action to this prudential end is an otherwise justified decision of what to do. And Kant so dealt with prudence, subsuming prudential rules and the prudential imperative under the hypothetical. But the prudential end, as he acknowledged, is happiness, the sum of all that men desire. And that concern, unlike any technical aim, is always with us and likely to be affected by any act whatever. Since any hypothetical directive becomes categorical when the "if" of it is satisfied, the prudential directives, whose "if" is that of wanting to be happy, have a force of "always" rather than of "when." In that sense, the prudential imperative is categorical rather than hypothetical. What Kant meant to insist upon is, of course, that although the prudential end is always desired, action by reference to it is far from being always justified, because the aim of prudence can be and should be overruled by that of justice when the two dictates are incompatible.

Granting, however, that justice has the precedent claim on action, there is still a further point of first importance. No concrete act can be so dictated by justice as to leave no feature of it undetermined and no remaining alternative of detail to be governed by prudence. I ought to pay my bill and satisfy my creditor; but payment by check or cash, today or the first of next month, may satisfy his just claim, and allow me justly to determine these alternatives by reference to any prudential consideration which may affect them. It lies in the fact that what any directive of right action will dictate is only a way of acting, and not some utterly specific doing, that prudence and justice, or any two diverse ends or grounds of right decision, may be coincidentally involved and be in whole or in part compatible. Furthermore, even when prudence is overruled, it still remains a valid concern, justly to be respected even though subordinated. As directive of such respect, the force of the prudential imperative, reflecting a pervasive and continuing concern, extends to every decision of action it could affect.

It is a shortcoming in ethics if the moralist, thinking to have elicited that overriding imperative to which any other must give way, forthwith dismisses directives of the right which are thus to be subordinated as if they had, in consequence, no significance for moral decisions of action and no import of the right and justified to do. It is even questionable to delimit the subject of morals by reference to any such categorical imperative which takes precedence. The total problem of right doing in any case, is of the same force and weight in all its parts; and to single out any one aspect as the moral import of it, and dismiss another aspect of the required decision as not a moral consideration, can be a prejudicial use of language. When it is not the whole of the specific act which need be dominated by the ruling requirement, the satisfaction of any which is subordinate remains as a valid demand of right doing calling for consideration in the decision to be taken. An act which is just to others but heedless of prudence is only part-way justified and is a wrong way to act.

There is, moreover, a relation between prudence and justice by reason of which it is fair to say that justice presupposes validity of the prudential aim. Without individual interests there could be no group or social interests, and without the validity of self-interests, no validity of any social interest. Society, as Herbert Spencer observed, has no central consciousness and can enjoy or suffer only in the persons of its members. All social categories are derivative—which is not to deny that they are distinct. Furthermore, justice is not to be confused with altruism. If justice requires giving weight to the interest of another equally as to one's own, that equation is also reversible and requires that one's own interest be weighed equally with that of any other. I would not say that benevolence beyond the call of justice has no sanction. There are goods of benevolence which may accrue to the benevolent individual himself. He may identify his own good with the good of those he serves, and find in that a deep self-interest. On that point, I would express my impressment with the ethics of self-realization. But the man of good will beyond the limit of obligation makes a gift, and it is to be appreciated as such and not construed as a requirement of the moral.

Our remaining questions are principally two: first, that concerning any sanction of justice by which it may override a prudential aim which conflicts; and second, observing that determination of the right turns upon such rules or principles only as are *valid,* the question what distinguishes valid principles, genuinely imperative to heed, from directives which are not thus valid. To ask this second question is, of course, to ask for the *ground* of such validity.

I would here discuss these two together, because it appears to me that the sanction of justice is the most obscure of all questions of ethics and that any illumination of it through consideration of the ground of right in general, if that be possible, would be a welcome kind of help.

Time out of mind, men have sought to find and demonstrate an ultimate ground of the right. But the right is *sui generis:* if the formulation of it be a kind of fact, still it is fact of a kind which is like no other; and what is right cannot be proved right by summoning premises which themselves say nothing about right and wrong. If there are any first principles of right, or first principles of the various categories of the right—and it is, of course, such first or most comprehensive principles which we should seek—it lies in the nature of the case that the validity of them will be indemonstrable. How prove valid the most general of all formulations of any given sort?

How, for example, should we prove any principles of logic which are basic and comprehensive enough to stand as first? We cannot derive statements of the logical from premises which themselves say nothing about the logical. And if, *per impossibile,* we could, we should still beg principles of logic as the only possible ground of correctness in this inference we make. Proof of a conclusion in logic calls not only for some assured premises of logic but also for demonstration of correctness in the proving. And proof of that kind of correctness can only be by appeal to logical principles, antecedently assured.

Or consider the question of demonstrating to a convinced Cynic the validity of the prudential aim so to act as to maximize the goodness realizable in a whole lifetime; or of proving this to one who holds the Benthamite principle of part-way prudence and is convinced that goods which are equally certain but more remote should weigh less heavily than nearer ones. We may truly say to one who flouts our correct principle of prudence, "You will be sorry someday"; but suppose he should answer, "So what? I'll be sorry when I get to it, but right now I'm having fun." We should be thrust back upon calling him perverse, silly, irrational; and these names would be appropriate, but they have no force of demonstration. Any attempt to induce recognition of principles of right as valid, can only appeal to some antecedent sense of such rightness which will, at some point, constrain any reasonable person to acknowledge them.

The ground of validity of imperatives must somehow lie in

our human nature. Human nature calls for principles of right decision. The necessity of that acknowledgment, if it should be challenged, must lie finally in the fact that to decide is unavoidable. Refusal to decide would be itself a decision. And one who in deciding should say, "I recognize no principles binding my decision," could be answered: "Let us be clear; just now you repudiate all principles, but that, I suppose, is only for the moment. Or do you repudiate principles, not by momentary whim, but as a matter of principle? Do you mean to make it a *principle* to have no principles?" He who adopts an active attitude constrains himself for the future. He who believes as true commits himself to continued belief so long as evidence remains the same, or otherwise, to acknowledge himself at fault in his belief. Consistency is first of attitude and prepared manner of response, and resistance to any changing whim of wishful thinking. The root of logic itself lies in the fact of decision, and decision as constraint upon future attitude.

Not only must we decide, and in decision find ourselves bound, but we must decide for some assignable reason. To decide but with no reason at all for so deciding, would be utterly to lose face with ourselves. That we must decide, and for a reason, is a distinctive feature of our human mentality. If we would put it in biological terms, we may observe that, having evolutionally outgrown exclusive government of our behavior by automatic response to stimuli and the way they make us feel, we are obliged to govern our doing, in part at least, by our thinking.

All thinking and, in consequence, all thoughtfully determined doing, exhibits two characteristics which are fundamental to the nature of it, namely, generality and objectivity. As we have already observed, generality is requisite because all learning and all knowing or knowing-how involves responding to a new and present situation in a manner reflective of the character of past like cases. Even the conditioned response of animals turns on that. And when thinking in part replaces such automatic response, it must still be general ways of thinking and ways of doing which we shall command and which will represent the modes in which any self-government is exercised. We must govern ourselves in definite ways which some elicitable rule could formulate.

What I would designate as objectivity is a character required by the fact that we live in time and the fact that it is the future only which can be affected—what is future in its impact on us, if not future in the occurrence of it. Thought and action are bent upon the future, to which alone any government or self-government can extend. That to which we must adapt is not immediate but something possible or to come and, so far as any activity is pertinent, possible to influence—possible to secure, to avert, to modify, or to prepare ourselves to meet. In our thinking, we must be impressed by something absent from the sensuously here and now and "realize" it as it will be when it comes. We must believe in what is not present but merely represented. And in our doing, we must respond to what is not felt but representationally intimated as we should respond if it were given with the poignancy of here and now. Only thus may we think as we shall later be satisfied to have thought and act so that later we shall not be sorry. However, to respond in this manner—directing ourselves to what is not immediate but with the same concern which we should have if we were immediately affected by it—requires on occasion some overriding of our animalish feeling which incites us to respond according to sensuous impact or emotive drive. That is the root of our sense of required constraint and of the imperative. And that is what is involved in our assignment of a reason for thinking or for deliberate doing. Our determination of the fact of what is absent from experience now, is what lies at the root of our reasoning. And our response governed by reference to non-immediate factualities, is our reasonable doing. To weigh the absent but represented in the *full-size* of it, and not in the measure of any presentational or emotive feeling which serves to intimate it, is to be objective. And to weigh it only in the measure of its immediate intimation as a present feeling, is to be subjective.

It is by reference to such objectivity in thought and action that, time out of mind, men have spoken of themselves as rational. And I see no reason to seek a different name for this distinctive feature of the human mentality. On this point, however, we have lived for two thousand years by ancient insights embedded in the idiom of our language; and in the process we may have come to substitute repetition of the familiar word for that self-understanding which the word was framed to convey. Perhaps it is time to replace the worn-out word by renewed grasp of the insight, and in terms which, conceivably, may better suit the context of the present. One thing we may need to observe is that the connotation of "reason" and "rationality" is not exclusively a reference to reasoning and valid inference. Correct inferring is only one side of this distinctive character of our mentality; only one aspect of being reasonable. A reason is a *consideration which justifies:* to have a sufficient reason for believing or for doing is to be justified in so deciding, and to have no reason is to be unjustified and non-rational or irrational.* It is recognition of imperatives as rational precepts which is the most general implication of human self-direction and self-constraint.

Let us try to suggest what lies at the root of all the imperatives of our thinking and doing as the Law of Objectivity: So conduct and determine your activities of thinking and of doing, as to conform any decision of them to the objective actualities, as cognitively signified to you in your representational apprehension of them, and not according to any impulsion or solicitation exercised by the affective quality of your present experience as immediate feeling merely.

Since so much of what should be decisive of thinking and of action concerns the future, let us add a corollary: Conduct yourself, with reference to those future eventualities which cognition advises that your activity may affect, as you would if these predictable effects of it were to be realized, at this moment of decision, with the poignancy of the here and now, instead of the less poignant feeling which representation of the future and possible may automatically arouse.

Does this Law of Objectivity have bearing upon that last and

---

* It may appear that "reason" in the sense of "a reason" has, as a second and unrelated meaning, the significance of "consideration which *explains*," either as cause or as law. Let us note, however, that whatever explains provides a ground for crediting as veridical—believing—in case of doubt. We trust an apprehension which might otherwise be dubious in measure as we find, e.g., a known cause of phenomena of the type in question which accords with laws which are known.

That feature which is common to all senses of "reason" is connotation of subsumption of the individual case, or the particular, under some generality.

most difficult question concerning justice to others, and the sanction of it as imperative? In this connection, we may do well to remember that the distinctively human mentality and the potentialities of it are hardly to be well observed if examination be restricted to the human animal as an individual organism merely. That of which man is capable, by reason of his peculiar endowment, can only be fully discovered by observation of him in society and in the history of the civilization he creates. Man is the only animal which *has* a history, the only species whose history is modified by his apprehension of it. Individuals of other species each begin where the preceding generation began, and their behavior is modifiable only by what they individually experience. But the generations of men begin where the preceding generation left off, profiting by the cumulative social recollection of what past generations have suffered and achieved. It is a basic consideration for the valid imperatives of individual human action, that the possibility of that kind of evolution which man alone exhibits, and of that progressive amelioration and enrichment of individual life found only in the human species, is conditional upon the modification of individual behavior by social agencies. Indeed it requires modification of the individual mentality itself, as to its grasp and content, as an effect of social relations—relationships which themselves similarly evolve, and whose evolution is by the same instrumentalities. The peculiarly human kind of life is *imperatively* social. That fact is a datum for ethics. To do justice to that topic would need a book—and books have, of course, been devoted to it.

The basic imperative for individuals in their relations to one another, is simply the socially significant counterpart of what we have observed already: the dictate to govern one's activities affecting other persons, as one would if these effects of them were to be realized with the poignancy of the immediate—hence, in one's own person. The dictate is to respect other persons as the realities we representationally recognize them to be —as creatures whose gratifications and griefs have the same poignant factuality as our own; and as creatures who, like ourselves, find it imperative to govern themselves in the light of the cognitive apprehensions vouchsafed to them, by decisions which they themselves reach, and by reference to values discoverable to them.

Perhaps we should divide this most general of moral principles into two. It has one part which turns only upon recognition of other creatures as being, like ourselves, subject to enjoyment and suffering. The dictate so derived may be called the Law of Compassion. And this same general principle of objectivity has another part or bearing which is relevant only in the case of other creatures who are like us also in their cognitive capacities and, in consequence, in the necessity of governing their own behavior by deliberation, and of acting under constraint of the imperatives of rationality. The dictate which is correlative here, we may call the Law of Moral Equality.

It is plain that the Law of Compassion extends not only to other humans but to all conscious beings in measure of that sentience we attribute to them as the capacity to find their experience satisfying or feel pain. Indeed this dictate of compassion is peculiarly in point in relation to those who are not our peers, but may lie within our power to help or harm in ways in which they cannot equally help themselves, or defend themselves against our intentions toward them. It applies to our conduct toward the lower animals. And it is also pertinent whenever our doing may affect humans who do not so fully realize the powers latent in human nature, and in those circumstances in which normal individuals may still not be able to exercise their normal capacities to the full. Again, and obviously, it applies to our conduct toward the immature, whose capacities have not yet fully ripened and been trained by the experience of life. This Law of Compassion must, I think, remain as an indeterminate duty to respect all conscious life for what it is, insofar as we are able to discern the nature of it as sentient. The question so involved whether every creature that enjoys and suffers, and not humans only, is so far an end in itself, is an infrequent topic in Western ethics. I shall not attempt elaboration of it here, or formulation of the law itself except as a general obligation: Recognize, in your action affecting any sentient being, that claim on your compassion which comports with its capacity to enjoy and suffer. Perhaps we shall agree at least that it is imperative, in any connection, to cause no useless pain.

The Law of Moral Equality shows, in some sense, the obverse of the Law of Compassion. It is peculiarly relevant to moral dealing with our full peers, and dictates respect for others not only as ends in themselves but as entitled to full self-determination of their individual action, to some privacy of decision, and to freedom from coercion in their decisions taken, so long as they bring no harm to others and accord to others a like freedom. But the morally more important implication lies in the fact that this Law of Moral Equality is likewise the principle of Equality before the Moral Law; the law that there shall be no law for one which is not law for all. This principle has joint implication with the fact that all self-government is government of *ways* of acting and by reference to statable rule. Both respect for others as our peers in self-determination under recognized imperatives, and the fact that self-determination can be exercised only by reference to some generality formulatable as a directive, have the consequence that no precept is valid and no mode of action is justified except as it is valid in the case of others as in our own. No manner of thought or action is valid for any of us except as, in the same premises of circumstance and evidenced fact, it is valid for all of us. This, be it noted, covers omissions to do as well as doing, since a decision not to do is a decision of action.

I regret to think that, for accuracy, this principle of Equality before the Moral Law must be stated in terms which will sound pedantic: Take no decision of action which is member of any class of decisions of doing all members of which you would call upon others to avoid. That is, I think, the intent of recognizing our own acts as right to do toward others only if we likewise acknowledge them as right when done to us. The particular points here are two: first, that rightness under rule is a matter of the classification or modes of acts; and second, that an act is right only if it falls in no class interdicted by rule. It is not sufficient that it exhibit *some* justifiable mode of action—be classified as doing of *some* sort, or acting in *some* way, which is morally permissible. What is essential is that it *not* be doing of *any* sort or acting in *any* way which is morally forbidden.

Our pedantic manner of formulation is dictated for the avoidance of two difficulties. First, there is the difficulty that a specious moralizer or a fanatic may elevate his selfish preference or one-sided interest to the status of a moral precept if allowed to do so on the ground of *his* willingness to see some mode of action universally permitted or made universally mandatory. Employers might so be free to accept it as a universal precept that wages paid should be minimal; and employees, that profits should be nil. And every bigot, content to see his particular bigotry become universal, could so justify himself in uninhibited imposition of it on others. But paying minimal wages is *also* imposing near-starvation; elimination of profits is *also* expropriation of the fruits of individual labor and saving; and the imposition of any bigotry is *also* the imposition of private opinion on others—ways of acting which no employer, no employee, and no bigot could be content to see become universal.

Second, and somewhat similarly, our mode of formulation avoids those too easy generalizations often found as maxims but untrustworthy if applied without common-sense qualification, and hence dangerous in the hands of the injudicious or of puritanical rigorists. The classic examples are "Tell no lies" and "Do not steal" which, though hardly to be excelled for moral guidance in common practice, are out of place in dealing with madmen bent on murder.

No rule of action can do more than divide all acts to which it could find application into two subclasses; those which, under this rule, are permissible, and those which contravene it and are impermissible. But an act is wrong if it contravenes *any* rule of right doing. And it is right only if it contravenes *no* rule of right doing. An act is wrong if it is wrong in *any* way; is any wrong way of acting. And it is right only if it is right in *every* way; if it is an act which in all respects is right to do. But if it be said that there are rules which categorically oblige some act, in all its particulars, then the answer is simply that this is not so. If it be a categorical moral command to pay our debts, what it commands is, "Choose *some* act, *some* way of acting, which will liquidate your debt." It is of some importance to observe that even the moral law leaves those who lie under its command some freedom of moral choice. Thus, logically viewed, the significance of "Do right" is "Do no wrong"; "Do nothing you would call upon others universally to avoid."

These principles, we may think, are basic for ethics. But lest the impression should have been given that, on the ground of them alone, we could straightway proceed to solution of all the major ethical problems, let us barely mention one such problem —or nest of problems—which we should encounter soon.

The Law of Moral Equality does not delineate the *content* of justice. For that, there are further facts of our common human nature which must be adduced, and further principles also which are hardly immediate inferences from those we have considered. For instance, the egoist as well as the social utilitarian can plausibly claim conformity to the principle of Equality under the Moral Law. In claiming prudence as the solely valid sanction for decisions of his own action, he likewise recognizes the moral correctness of others in so deciding theirs. He claims that egoistic conduct is *just*. If there is a basic principle of morals which he affronts, it is the Law of Compassion. But a Bentham or a Hume would be sure to counter by the observation that compassion is a native human propensity and as rational and "selfish" to indulge in as any other. It is more plausible to suppose that universal egoism is contra-indicated by the egoist's misapprehensions concerning the pos-

sibilities of a good life for anybody under conditions of uninhibited egoism. On that point, Hobbes seems more convinc-
ing; in such a state of nature life would be "nasty, brutish, and
short."

But on the other hand, would life in a society of perfect
altruists afford optimum conditions for individual happiness?
Not, I should suppose, in view of our actual human nature.
One of the major goods of life is liberty to decide private matters on private grounds, without paternalistic oversight, and
with the privilege of making our own mistakes. We even—
most of us—cherish some privilege of competition with our
fellows, within the bounds of our over-all social cooperation;
and we think that allowance, or even encouragement, of certain modes of competition is essential to progress and conducive
to the general welfare. But a mode of activity is competitive
only insofar as individual prudential ends are put in front
of any equal consideration of the good of others affected, and
only so far as the success of one participant or party militates
against the like success of others.

The content of social justice, it is suggested, requires to be
determined in view of additional premises concerning human
nature and human good which are empirical generalizations
rather than principles of the type so far cited. There may be also,
contained in such considerations, the suggestion that any posi-
tive ethics may find itself in like case on other points. In particular, it may be suggested that the grounds of the cooperation of individuals in society, for the sake of the common good,
and the ground on which dictates essential to the maintenance
of effective cooperation are imperatives for individual conduct,
would be among the problems to be so probed.

If, in conclusion, we look briefly to the general character of any ethic which should conform to the general conclusions here reached, we may observe that it would be of that type usually called naturalistic, so far as it is classified by reference to the thesis that no act can be determined as right or wrong without reference to consequences of it as good or bad. Also, it would be naturalistic in its interpretation of good and bad as matters of empirical fact and as significant, at bottom, of naturally found qualities of experience. It would, however, have a character frequently taken to be antithetic to naturalism; namely, in the thesis that right and wrong are nevertheless indeterminable except by reference of rules or principles—principles themselves including reference to the good or bad as essential to determining what specifically they dictate. It would likewise be liable to classification as antithetic to naturalism in its conclusion that these imperatives of right, and the validity of them, have no other determinable and final ground than that character of human nature by which it is called rational. However, if a view incorporating both sets of these features can be consistently maintained, then what so appears is that ethical naturalism and ethical rationalism (if "rationalism" is the right word here) are not in fact antithetic but complementary. Perhaps they are antithetic only for a naturalism which connotes nature short of human nature, or for a rationalism which interprets rationality as non-natural and significant of some transcendent world.